Bernat Metge
Book of Fortune and Prudence

Bernat Metge
Book of Fortune and Prudence

Introduced and translated by
David Barnett

BARCINO · TAMESIS

BARCELONA/WOODBRIDGE 2011

First published 2011
by Tamesis (Serie B: TEXTOS, 55)
in association with Editorial Barcino

LLLL institut
ramon llull
Catalan Language and Culture

The translation of this work has been supported
by a grant from the Institut Ramon Llull

ISBN 978 1 855662 285
COPYRIGHT DEPOSIT: B-17.640-2011

Tamesis is an imprint of Boydell & Brewer Ltd
PO Box 9, Woodbridge, Suffolk IP12 3DF, UK
and of Boydell & Brewer Inc.
668 Mt Hope Avenue, Rochester, NY 14620, USA
www.boydellandbrewer.com

Editorial Barcino, S. A.
Acàcies 15. 08027 Barcelona, Spain
www.editorialbarcino.cat

Designed and typeset by Jordi Casas

Printed in Spain by Gràfiko

Cover illustration:
Pere Niçard and Rafael Moguer,
Harbour of the City of Mallorca
Detail of the Altarpiece of Saint George
Last third of fifteenth century
(Museu Diocesà de Mallorca)

Contents

Introduction

Bernat Metge's fame is as a writer of prose. *The Dream* (*Lo somni*), Metge's final (extant) work written just before the turn of the fifteenth century when the author was in his fifties, is widely considered to be one of the prose masterpieces of Catalan medieval literature. Given that it has only recently been translated into English for the first time, it is clear that Henry Chaytor's comment in the 1930s that Metge 'deserves more fame than he has obtained' is still valid, at least outside Catalonia.[1] The *Book of Fortune and Prudence* (*Llibre de Fortuna i Prudència*), in contrast to *The Dream,* is in verse and dates from the 1380s, when Metge was in his early thirties. It is one of his earliest surviving works and, as such, has inevitably been compared with *The Dream.* The negative connotations implicit in many comparisons between an author's mature work and his early output are compounded in Metge's case by the association of his later prose with Petrarch and the pre-Renaissance, and his earlier verse with quintessentially medieval and so somewhat backward-looking literary traditions. However, as scholars have deepened their study of the *Book of Fortune and Prudence* in recent decades, the work has been and is still being reappraised. New information about Metge's access to possible source texts, and analyses of how he used those texts, have helped to refine our evaluation of how

---

[1]Richard Vernier, trans., *The Dream of Bernat Metge* (Burlington, VT: Ashgate, 2002). Henry J. Chaytor, *A History of Aragon and Catalonia* (London: Methuen, 1933), p. 199.

the work fits into the rich tradition of allegorical-philosophical narratives. Many of the canonical works of the genre from the Middle Ages
use the same sources. This practice, to a modern readership, might
smack of plagiarism or a lack of either originality or creativity. However, such notions of copying were alien to the contemporary readership. That said, authors clearly engaged with former texts in varying
degrees: some did little more than translate or paraphrase, while others treated their source materials with more freedom, originality or
deftness. In an echo of Chaytor's comments, John Fleming closes his
1982 article by pointing out that Metge's poem 'deserves rather more
praise than it has received', in particular for his subtle handling of the
core texts of the Boethian tradition.[2]

Metge was Barcelona born and bred. The *Book of Fortune and Prudence* opens with the first-person narrator, perhaps Metge himself, wak-
ing early on a spring day in 1381. As he heads to the shore to clear his
head, we become aware that the location is Barcelona—and this is con-
firmed at the very end of the work. The city in the late fourteenth century occupied an area slightly smaller than today's Gothic Quarter
(*Barri Gòtic*), and was a key Mediterranean port.[3] It was the commercial
and administrative centre of the Crown of Aragon.[4] There were no
Ramblas—the famous boulevard was at that time the site of the medieval city walls—and the streets, in particular around the port, were
bustling with foreign merchants rather than tourists. There was plenty
of building activity: many of the city's churches, palaces and civic build-
ings were undergoing extensive renovations and expansions. Jousting
contests were held in the Born district, where people met to eat, drink

[2] John Fleming, 'The Major Source of Bernat Metge's *Libre de Fortuna e Prudència*',
Journal of Hispanic Philology 7 (Fall 1982), p. 13.

[3] In terms of surface area, Barcelona was about a third of the size of Venice, half that
of Paris, and just a little larger than London. It had a population of about 30,000, well
below the 200,000 of the more densely populated Paris or the 100,000 of Venice, but
again comparable with London (figures taken from Jaume Sobrequés i Callicó's *Història
de Barcelona* [Barcelona: Plaza Janés, 2008], p. 71).

[4] The Crown of Aragon was a medieval kingdom that by the late fourteenth century
stretched from Zaragoza in the west, just beyond Alicante in the south, to Perpignan in
the north and eastwards across the Mediterranean. The origins of this vast kingdom lie
in a marriage in the mid-twelfth century between the Count of Barcelona and the daughter of the Aragonese king. This union spawned a dynasty that ruled without interruption
until the early fifteenth century. See T.N. Bisson, *The Medieval Crown of Aragon: A Short History* (Oxford: Clarendon, 1986), and David Abulafia, *The Western Mediterranean Kingdoms
1200-1500: The Struggle for Dominion* (London & New York: Longman, 1997).

and socialise. Religious festivals and royal occasions were celebrated with noisy and colourful processions. However, in the 1380s, there were signs of troubled times ahead. Previously lucrative trade routes were being disrupted by war in the West and the East. Poor harvests and several devastating outbreaks of the plague in the mid-1300s had reduced the population, with consequences for productivity, the markets and trade. Across Europe, the poor bore the brunt of the economic downturn as the aristocracy sought to preserve its position of privilege: the Revolt of the Ciompi in Florence in 1378 and the Peasant's Revolt in England in 1380 are examples of the cracks that were starting to appear in the feudal system. In Barcelona, relations between the monarchy and the municipal institutions were becoming strained. The economic problems affecting much of the Western World were exacerbating a local cash-flow problem centred on one of the city's main banking houses which had particularly close ties with the royal treasury. In March 1381 the bank ceased trading; several other banking houses collapsed in the next two years in other Catalan cities.[5]

In 1381, King Peter IV (1319-87) was on the throne. He earned his sobriquet 'the Ceremonious' because of his extensive reforms of the bureaucracy that supported the royal court. It is partly due to these reforms that the Archive of the Crown of Aragon is today one of the richest medieval record repositories in the world.[6] Maintaining such a remarkable feat of record-keeping required a body of highly-skilled, well educated and literate functionaries. They acquired expertise in drafting letters and documents in the three official languages of the kingdom—Latin, Catalan and Aragonese—through a five-year-long apprenticeship that involved reading and studying a range of texts. In the hierarchy of the royal chancery, the very brightest functionaries who rose to the top had unparalleled access to, and enjoyed the trust of, the royal family. Bernat Metge occupied such a post for much of his adult life.

---

[5] For further information on the economic crisis, see Angus MacKay, *Spain in the Middle Ages: From Frontier to Empire, 1000-1500* (London: Macmillan, 1977), pp. 165-68. On the banking crisis, see Manuel Riu, 'Banking and Society in Late Medieval and Early Modern Aragon' in *The Dawn of Modern Banking* (New Haven & London: Yale University Press, 1979), pp. 131-67.

[6] For example, for Peter's rule alone (1336-87) there are over 1,200 volumes of records (200 pages per volume), nearly 3,500 parchment documents, and a further 7,500 on paper.

Biography

Bernat Metge was born in the late 1340s, just a few years later than
Chaucer, into a family with royal connections. His father, Guillem
Metge, was a pharmacist who attended to the medical needs of King
Peter's third wife, Elionor of Sicily, and those of her household, pre-
sumably including the young Prince John, the king's eldest son, heir
apparent, and future King John I (1350-96). Guillem died in 1359
while Bernat was barely a teenager. Five years later, his widow, Agnès,
remarried one of her first husband's colleagues, Ferrer Saiol, employed
at Elionor's court as a scribe and promoted the following year (1365)
to her chief secretary or protonotary (*protonotari*). Ferrer's incorpora-
tion into the Metge household was to have important implications for
Bernat's career. In 1370, aged around 25, Bernat had completed his
apprenticeship—almost certainly with his stepfather—and was working as a royal notary. The following year (1371), he was promoted to
the post of registry assistant (*ajudant de registre*) in Elionor's household.
When she died in 1375, Bernat continued in royal service, but in the
household of Prince John. He remained there, working first as a scribe,
and then, following John's accession to the throne in 1387, as his secretary from 1390 onwards.

From a very early age, therefore, Metge would have been familiar
with the workings of the court, originally from his father's contact with
Elionor, and then later through his stepfather Ferrer's more prominent
role in the same household. In those pre-university days—the first Catalan university was founded in 1300 in Lleida, but it would be the mid-
fifteenth century before there was one in Barcelona—, the royal court
was an important centre of learning. Prior to the establishment of the
royal chancery, knowledge of Latin had been the preserve of the Church.
The rise of an entire army of bureaucrats who were, by profession, ex-
perts in reading and drafting documents in Latin and the vernacular is
directly related to the increase in the second half of the fourteenth century of translations of secular Latin classics, commissioned by the court.
Although at one remove from the principal European cultural centres
of the time—Paris, Avignon, Florence, Venice—the royal family were
themselves highly educated and well read, and had the means and connections to pursue their literary interests.

Two anecdotal but well-documented incidents illustrate the cultural emphasis in courtly life, and Metge's involvement in it. Trouba-

dour poetry, written in a Catalan that betrays a strong Provençal influence, was popular among the aristocracy in the second half of the fourteenth century. Interchanges or dialogues in troubadouresque verse were held between members of the royal family, including King Peter himself. These exchanges would then be commented on and discussed at court. After one such exchange in 1374, the king's son, Prince John, wrote to Ferrer Saiol, Metge's stepfather, asking for his impressions concerning the impact his works had had on the king and queen. This illustrates not only the importance at court of the Gay Science, as the troubadour's art was known, but also the key role that chancery staff played in such exchanges. John turned to a scribe employed in his parents' household for information on cultural matters. Similarly, just over twenty years later, in 1395, while John—now King John—was spending the summer months in Mallorca to avoid the plague on the mainland, he lent his secretary, Metge, who was accompanying him on his sojourn, a copy of Cicero's *Somnium Scipionis* (*The Dream of Scipio*), so that he could read it and then be in a position to discuss it with the king. These examples give us an idea of the literary tastes of members of the court, both as readers and writers. Furthermore, they also show the way in which the king's closest advisors were consulted not just on political and diplomatic issues, but literary matters too.

John, both as a prince and when he became king, was well known for his love of the arts, especially music, and of hunting. His second marriage in 1380—his first wife had died in childbirth two years earlier—to the precocious 15-year-old Yolande of Bar, the daughter of Robert, Duke of Bar, and Maria, sister of Charles V of France, provided the court with a direct channel to one of the key European cultural centres. From the wealth of epistolary exchanges preserved in the Archive of the Crown of Aragon, we know that the frequent requests made by the Catalan prince and his new wife for specific books from the royal French libraries were often answered. This French influence is of key importance when we come to look at the sources of Metge's *Book of Fortune and Prudence*. John's connections with France and French culture can be traced back to his parents, and to his two marriages, and one unsuccessful engagement, all to French princesses. He spoke French and enjoyed reading French from an early age; French musicians and poets were employed at his court; and his enthusiasm for one of the great French cultural exports of the time—Arthurian romances—is reflected in the names he gave to his dogs: Tristan and

Merlin. Note also, that it is through this French influence in the Aragonese court that Latin classics come to be known. In this respect Charles V and another of Yolande of Bar's uncles, the Duke of Berry, are key figures, furnishing Catalan translators with French versions of Latin works (Livy, Seneca, and Valerius Maximus, among others).

Throughout John I's reign, Metge was a key player at court. As a trusted confidant of the king and queen, he accompanied them wherever they travelled, and was occasionally despatched abroad on diplomatic missions. The royal court, however, was mired in accusations of corruption and the mismanagement of funds. Distrust of the king and his advisors by the elected urban councils of Barcelona and Valencia led to open hostility between city councils and the royal chancery. On May 18 1396, in the midst of a particularly frenetic series of highly-charged exchanges between the king, his chancery, and members of the Barcelona Council, John I died suddenly, allegedly while out hunting. Maria de Luna, the wife of John I's brother, Martin, assumed the throne in her husband's name. Many of the deceased king's advisors, including Metge, were rounded up and charged. Some were imprisoned, others put under house arrest. A year later, King Martin I, 'the Humane', arrived in Barcelona and freed all the prisoners. The following year the defendants were acquitted of all charges. It is around this time (1399), and in this context, that Metge wrote what is widely considered his masterpiece, and one of the most celebrated works in prose from the Crown of Aragon: *The Dream*.

By 1402, Metge was clearly back in royal favour as he was employed within Martin I's royal chancery. He was promoted to the king's secretary in 1405, a post he retained until the king died without a successor in 1410. Metge himself died three years later.

Other works

Seven works by Metge have survived, three in verse, and four in prose. Another work, *Lucidari*, probably also in prose, is mentioned in a 1444 inventory but is no longer extant. The exact chronology of his oeuvre is difficult to establish as only two works—the *Book of Fortune and Prudence* and *The Dream* — can be dated with any certainty. Nevertheless, it does seem likely that his verse works are from the earlier part of his career.

The *Book of Fortune and Prudence* is the longest of Metge's three verse works. The other two, *Sermon* (*Sermó*) and *Medicine suitable for all ills* (*Medecina apropiada a tot mal*) are both much shorter, both playfully satirical, and may both predate the *Book of Fortune*. The first of these, a poem of 211 lines in *codolada* (a long line followed by a short line, rhyming), is a litany of impious maxims parodying contemporary sermons. The tone is similar to that of boy-bishop sermons, but somewhat more cynical and ascerbic.[7] The second, *Medicine suitable for all ills*, consists of 125 octosyllabic couplets. The work is written in the first person and is in the form of a letter sent by the author-narrator from prison to an ailing friend, called Bernat.[8] It's a mock prescription which claims to aid his friend's recovery, in humorous imitation of the electuaries (*lletovaris*) penned by poets to cure love sickness. It also satirises medieval pharmaceutical practices and jargon, with which Metge was familiar from his early childhood and adolescence spent with his father. We find the themes of consolation and counsel in both these works recurring in the *Book of Fortune*.

It is thought that Metge's prose translation of part of the Pseudo-Ovidian *De vetula* (*On the Old Woman*), attributed by some scholars to Richard de Fournival, is also an early work. It necessarily predates *The Dream* which includes a quotation from it. This light-hearted, bawdy story tells of how an old woman takes the place of the object of the narrator's desires and thus tricks him into sleeping with her. Metge's version, *Ovid in love* (*Ovidi enamorat*), is a translation of most of the second book, in which he changes the first-person narrator of the original into the third-person Ovid. One of the reasons why this is considered an early work is that the quality of the translation—which features some curious Latinisms—is clearly inferior to another prose translation he

---

[7] In churches and monasteries throughout Europe in the Middle Ages and later, a boy was elected 'bishop' (*episcopus puerorum* or, in Catalan, *bisbetó*) on the feast of St Nicholas (6 December) and assumed the role, seated on a throne complete with mitre and crosier, on 27/28 December (Holy Innocents' Day) when he gave an often humorous sermon, supposedly as a child who had escaped from the Massacre of the Innocents. In England, the boy-bishop often swapped places with the real bishop during the *Magnificat*, at the lines 'He hath put down the mighty from their seat, and hath exalted the humble and meek'. Riquer points out that there is a coincidence between a few lines at the end of Metge's work and one of two extant boy-bishop sermons in Catalan (*Història de la literatura catalana* [Barcelona: Ariel, 1964], vol. 3, p. 43).

[8] Some scholars have suggested the friend may be Bernat Margarit, one of John I's early councillors, who was also charged in 1396 following the king's death. If this hypothesis were correct, the work would have to be dated much later, to the late 1390s.

carried out in around 1388. Metge's *Walter and Griselda* (*Història de Valter e Griselda*) was a Catalan prose version of Petrarch's revised *Griseldis* (1374, first version 1373), itself a translation of the tenth and final story from the tenth day of Boccaccio's *Decameron* (1350-53).[9] The story tells of how Walter, the marquis of Saluzzo, grudgingly accepts his subjects' exhortations to marry and chooses the daughter of a peasant whom he notices while out hunting. On the day designated for the wedding the marquis and his entourage arrive at the peasant's village and, once he has obtained the father's permission, he has his daughter Griselda brought out, stripped in public, and then dressed in finery and led away to married life. The remaining narrative details the extreme and ultimately unnecessary ways in which Walter tests Griselda's fidelity and loyalty: he leads her to believe that he has killed their two children, then deceives her into believing that he has secured a papal bull to annul their marriage and intends to remarry; and he expects her to make the wedding preparations. Griselda bears all these trials with exemplary steadfastness, so much so, that the marquis finally reveals, on his second wedding day, that his supposed bride to be is in fact their daughter. The family is reunited and the tale finishes with a conventional happy ending.

Petrarch (1304-74) revised his original translation shortly before his death and included it in his *Rerum senilium* (*Letters of old age*), between two letters to his friend Boccaccio. Metge also included his *Walter and Griselda* in a letter to Isabel de Guimerà, the daughter of Berenguer de Relat (d. 1390), head of the royal finances (*mestre racional*), whom Metge must have met and befriended when he was working as a registry assistant in Elionor's household. His lengthy opening remarks and shorter farewell not only incorporate some of Petrarch's comments addressed to Boccaccio, but also include his enthusiastic evaluation of the works of the great Italian humanist, the first such comments in the vernacular in the Iberian Peninsula.[10] That Metge had read and appreciated Petrarch's

---

[9] The *Decameron* is a collection of 100 novellas, placed within a narrative frame in which a group of ten friends flee a plague-ridden Florence to a country villa where they while away ten days telling stories. The final story of Griselda, told by Dioneo, is among the most popular, partly because of Petrarch's translation. There are three other contemporary vernacular versions of the tale: two in French, the earlier by Philippe de Mézières (1327-1405), which Metge consulted when writing his version, and the other anonymous; and one by Chaucer, the narrative of the *Clerk's Tale* in the *Canterbury Tales*.

[10] King John I's scribe, Pere de Pont, is the first Iberian to praise Petrarch's works in Latin a year or so before.

work (in Latin, rather than his vernacular poetry) barely 15 years after his death is a telling indication of the level of Metge's learning and intellect and the extent to which the Aragonese chancery kept abreast of contemporary literary currents.

His translation of this typically medieval moral tale, or *exemplum*, is notable for its precision, a reflection of Metge's professional notarial training. The epistolary frame, however, is written in a more complex and florid prose that anticipates the mature style of *The Dream*, and before that, the *Apology* (*Apologia*). Only a fragment of this dialogue has survived—the only extant manuscript witness breaks off mid-sentence. It connects the author once again with Petrarch: Metge was sent to Avignon as part of an ambassadorial mission in 1395 and it is likely that while he was there he read Petrarch's *Secretum* (written in Latin 1347-53), a dream in which the author dialogues with St Augustine in the presence of Truth personified. The *Apology* is Metge's attempt at imitating the *Secretum*, at writing in a classical genre: the philosophical dialogue, associated with Plato and Cicero. Like the *Book of Fortune and Prudence*, it is written in the first person and at the start of the text the author-narrator is at home in Barcelona, where he receives a visit from a friend, with whom he starts to chat about the recent plague. There is enough in the couple of pages of this fragment, however, to show that this is from a different, later period of Metge's work.

Metge wrote *The Dream* in the first quarter of 1399, some four years after the presumed date of the *Apology*. In the opening lines of the *Book of Fortune and Prudence* and the epistolary prologue to his *Walter and Griselda*, the author-narrator is in some sort of trouble, although the precise nature of his predicament is not specified. At the start of *The Dream*, and *Medicine suitable for all ills*, the narrator is in prison. We should, nevertheless, approach these statements with extreme caution and be wary of drawing conclusions from them about the author's biography. A standard component of works such as these that can be ascribed to the *consolatio* genre was a *lamentatio* in which the narrator bemoans his current misfortune. Contemporary documentation indicates that Metge was charged in two separate court cases, one in 1388 (coinciding with *Walter*) and the other in 1396 (*The Dream*), but there is no evidence that he was imprisoned on either occasion.

The work is also written in the first person. It is divided into four books, and the principal form throughout is the dialogue, modelled on Cicero. In the first, the author-narrator (Bernat, from here on) is surprised in his prison cell by the arrival of King John I accompanied by the seer Tiresias, Orpheus, the musician, and a pack of hunting dogs. An incredulous Bernat asks how the dead king came to be there. John explains that his body has died but not his soul, prompting a discussion, that borrows from an impressive range of classical sources, in which the king persuades Bernat to abandon his initial scepticism concerning the immortality of the soul. Note that from the reader's point of view, Bernat's scepticism is far more convincing than his subsequent change of heart. In the second book, more sparing in its use of sources, we learn that John is in Purgatory, and that his entourage has been assembled in accordance with the excesses he confessed to in life: Tiresias for his taste for astrological predictions, Orpheus for his love of music, and the dogs for his passion for hunting. The remainder of the book focuses more on contemporary events and personalities, and is a poorly disguised attempt by Bernat to ingratiate himself with the new king, John's brother, Martin I. Bernat pleads his innocence, praises the royal family, but rather muddies the waters by appearing to criticise John—and by extension Martin himself—for supporting the Avignon pope.[11] In the third book, Tiresias and Orpheus tell their respective stories, before the subject matter turns to a more personal episode in the author-narrator's life, namely an affair with a woman who was not his wife. This prompts a vicious misogynist diatribe based on Boccaccio's *Corbaccio* (1355). In the fourth and final book, an attempt is made to redress the balance following this invective by eulogising a host of women stretching back through classical times right up to contemporary queens, lavishing especially kind words on Maria de Luna, Martin I's wife.

[11] Seven popes, with close ties to the French royal court, presided over the papal Curia at Avignon from 1305 to 1377, when Pope Gregory XI returned to Rome. Following his death in 1378, the papal conclave first elected an Italian pope, Urban VI, then, five months later, a French one, Clement VII. For the next twenty years, during the so-called Western Schism, there were two popes: one in Rome, recognised by Flanders, England, and northern Italian states; and another in Avignon, supported by Aragon, Castile and Leon, southern Italian states, and, until 1398, France. The Schism was resolved during the Council of Constance (1414-18): the Roman pope Gregory XII resigned and when the Aragonese-born Avignon pope Benedict XIII refused to do so, he was excommunicated. The Council elected a new pope, Martin V. In the early years of the Schism, Peter IV of Aragon had remained neutral. However, his son, John I, after extensive consultations, declared his support for the Avignon papacy. Martin I continued to support the increasingly divisive Benedict XIII, even after the withdrawal of French support for the Avignon branch in 1398.

The work is deservedly held in high esteem as one of the treasures of medieval Catalan literature. It is complex and enigmatic, witty and entertaining. The prose is elegant and polished. Martin I requested a copy of the work in April 1399. If its primary intention was to curry favour with the new royal incumbent, it clearly worked: Metge was back in a position of responsibility within the chancery in less than a couple of years.

Book of Fortune and Prudence

In lines 26-28 of the *Book of Fortune and Prudence* Metge gives the date of the narrative action as 1 May 1381. This is the only dating evidence we have for the work, and it is assumed that he wrote it shortly after that date. The work is written in octosyllabic rhyming couplets (aabbcc, *noves rimades* in Catalan), a form used for narrative verse from the thirteenth to the fifteenth centuries. There are no stanza breaks in the manuscripts.

Manuscripts

There are two extant manuscripts of the *Book of Fortune and Prudence*, both in the Biblioteca de Catalunya, Barcelona, and both dating from the first half of the fifteenth century. In one, Biblioteca de Catalunya, MS 8 (the second volume of the Cançoner Vega-Aguiló), the text has been copied alongside other comparable verse narratives as part of a songbook miscellany which includes Metge's own *Sermon*, and Guillem de Torroella's *The Tale* (*La faula*). This can be dated to between 1417 and 1430. The other manuscript, Biblioteca de Catalunya, MS 831, is a collection of Metge's satirical works: it contains parts of *The Dream*, all of his *Sermon*, the only manuscript witness of *Ovid in love*, and the *Book of Fortune and Prudence* (missing the first 119 lines). The manuscript has been dated to the middle of the fifteenth century, perhaps the 1440s, and appears to have been compiled for personal use. Both manuscripts derive more or less directly from an earlier manuscript, now lost. The first of these two manuscripts is used as the base text for the edition in this translation.

It was rediscovered in the modern era at the end of the nineteenth century by the Catalan scholar Milà i Fontanals, who gave it its title.

The first modern edition is from 1910 and it has been re-edited more than a dozen times since. It has been translated into Spanish.[12]

Synopsis

In a brief introduction (ll. 1-25), the author-narrator (Bernat) explains that he does not want the current difficulties he finds himself in to prevent him from telling the story of his adventure. The attentive reader will learn from it about the vagaries of Fortune. He closes his opening remarks with a conventional apology for the length of his tale, and his lack of expertise in writing verse.

The narrative proper begins: Bernat wakes up before dawn on 1 May 1381 feeling unwell. To alleviate his symptoms, he decides to go for a walk along the seafront, where he immediately feels better (26-47). He sees an old man sitting on the dockside, naked. Thinking he is a beggar, Bernat offers him money. The old man refuses but asks him to bring him a cape he left on the boat that brought him there. As soon as he boards the boat, the old man launches it with only Bernat on board, and no oars, sails or rudder (48-91). Vowing to exact revenge on the old man at a later date, he is carried along through a storm before the weather calms and—to his great relief— he catches sight of land (92-149). He leaps from the boat onto a rocky island, at first sight uninhabited. His mood swings from delight to apprehension: to explain why, he offers a description of the island (150-85).

In a lengthy poetical passage, he describes the abrupt and frequent changes in climate (186-213), the flora and fauna which seem to defy the laws of nature (214-47), and the contrasting properties of the island's two rivers (248-87). He climbs to a high vantage point from which he can see a castle, sumptuously decorated on one side, but covered in filth on the other (288-313).

Bernat's heart sinks even further as he comes face to face with the castle's inhabitant: Fortune herself. He describes her as exceptionally ugly. Her face is on the back of her head (the front is covered in hair), her eyes are quite different one from the other, and her attire is de-

---

[12] Riquer's 1959 edition of the complete works of Bernat Metge, *Obras de Bernat Metge* (Barcelona: Universitat de Barcelona), also contains a Spanish translation.

ceptive in that the expensive-looking outer garments hide the poor rags underneath. She is lame, with a hunchback and arms of different lengths, and constantly passes a wheel from one hand to the other. Bernat falls to the ground, terrified (314-73).

She asks him to stand and then introduces herself, detailing her ability to dispense good or bad fortune wherever she pleases. Bernat blames her for his recent troubles, bemoans his current predicament, and rails against her for picking on him unfairly (374-541). She defends her actions, explaining that she only ever takes away what she has first freely bestowed. To back up her defence, she draws parallels with the extortionate banking practices of the time (542-89). The exchange ends with mutual recriminations, bad-tempered name-calling, and Fortune hurling Bernat through the air. He lands and loses consciousness (590-643).

When he comes to, he sees a beautiful lady accompanied by seven well-dressed women. She introduces herself as Prudence and her entourage as the Liberal Arts. She declares that he is critically ill, but that she can cure him. He is, according to her, suffering from ignorance in that he believes Fortune to be to blame for his condition (644-727). His treatment is administered through a complex philosophical dialogue in which Prudence argues that if God created the world, as Bernat believes, Fortune cannot have the power she claims. Bernat accepts this point, but argues that God is unjust because He allows people to commit wrongdoing (728-85). Prudence defends God's judgment, criticising Bernat for equating material wealth with goodness, and reminding him that doing good works, enduring suffering with patience, and loving God are the keys to Paradise (786-891). Prudence then goes on to contrast human judgment, necessarily subjective and therefore flawed, with omniscient divine judgment, which is always governed by reason, even if that reason is not always apparent to humankind (892-977). To illustrate this point, she provides a catalogue of examples, and analyses of the excellence of divine judgment which is beyond human comprehension. She concludes her argument by declaring that evil is the absence of good, an absence of something is nothing, man's wrongdoing is therefore nothing, so Fortune is always good (978-1105). Recommending Bernat to show patience in his dealings with Fortune, she declares him cured of his ailment and excuses herself because she is very busy (1106-47).

Prudence and the Liberal Arts return him to his boat, bid him farewell, and send him on his way. He is transported back to where his journey started. As soon as he disembarks, the boat vanishes. It is not yet dawn, and he hurries back to his house in Barcelona (1148-94).

Sources

Metge's *Book of Fortune and Prudence* belongs to a rich medieval genre: the allegorical-philosophical narrative poem. It is inspired by French narrative poems, such as the *Roman de Philosophie* (late twelfth century) by Simon de Freine, and the *Roman de Fauvel* (1314) by Gervais de Bus, and shares the tradition with, among others, Dante's *Divine Comedy* from the early fourteenth century, as well as *Piers Ploughman* and *The Pearl*, from the second half of the fourteenth century, all of which use allegory and personification to discuss abstract and philosophical questions. In this it is clearly indebted to four immediate key sources: *The Consolation of Philosophy* by Boethius, *Elegia* by Henry of Settimello, *Anticlaudianus* by Alan of Lille, and the *Romance of the Rose* by Guillaume de Lorris and Jean de Meun, the first three in Latin and the last in French.

Boethius (c. 480-c. 525) was a highly educated man, who held the offices of consul and head of the civil service (*magister officiorum*), but whose real passion was philosophy which he studied throughout his life. He is a key figure in philosophy partly because of his crucial role in transmitting Aristotle's logic—through his translations of and commentaries on his work—and partly for his systematic ordering of classical philosophical thought which heralded a new approach to the subject, Scholasticism. His last work, *The Consolation of Philosophy*, is his most famous: according to C.S. Lewis, 'for centuries one of the most influential books ever written in Latin'.[13] It was translated, annotated and imitated countless times in the Middle Ages and early modern period. Chaucer, for example, translated it (*Boece*, consulting Jean de Meun's French translation in the process), and used it as a source for the passage on the philosophy of love in *Troilus and Criseyde*; it is the inspiration for the fifteenth-century poem *The Kingis Quair*, attributed to James I of Scotland, and another monarch, Elizabeth I, is reputed to

[13] *The Discarded Image* (Cambridge: Cambridge University Press, 1964), p. 75.

have translated it in under 30 hours. And it is this work that is the main source for Metge's *Book of Fortune and Prudence*.

Boethius fell out of favour in the 520s for espousing a political stance no longer sanctioned by the emperor Theodoric the Great and the Roman Senate: he was sent into exile in Pavia, tortured, and executed. He wrote *The Consolation of Philosophy* while in prison, awaiting execution. It belongs to the classical genre of *consolatio*, which had a variety of forms, but a single aim: to provide the reader with solace at a time of distress. Boethius's work alternates between verse and prose. He deftly combines a wide range of sources, styles, and philosophical approaches. He begins by bemoaning his fall from grace and his current bad fortune; he is consoled by the allegorical figure of Philosophy, on whom Metge based his Prudence; and the main body of the text is a sacred dialogue which includes an extended medical metaphor—also adopted by Metge—as Philosophy diagnoses and treats Boethius's illness by underlining the ethereal nature of worldly fame and glory. At the heart of Boethius's *Consolation* lies a theodicy: a justification for the existence of a supremely good Godhead in a world where evil exists, a way of marrying the two apparently contradictory principles of free will and divine omnipotence. As Watts points out, Boethius's argument appears forced to a modern readership with its insistence on the fixed and inflexible meaning of words: 'the argument ... that "evil is nothing" on the grounds that "God who can do all things cannot do evil" and that "what God cannot do is nothing", and the further conclusion that evil men are powerless, will fail to convince'.[14] This same typically Scholastic line of argumentation underpins the dialogue between the narrator and Prudence in the *Book of Fortune and Prudence*. And aside from the obvious influence of Boethius on the basic structure and premise of Metge's work, much of the central section of Metge's text (the dialogue with Prudence) follows the thread of Book IV of Boethius very closely.

Boethius—'the last of the Romans and the first of the scholastics'[15]—is a bridging figure, assimilating classical literary and philosophical texts in a way that clearly appealed to a medieval readership. Henry of Settimello's 1,000-line poem, *Elegia*, written in the early

[14] V.E. Watts, ed., *Boethius: The Consolation of Philosophy* (London: Penguin, 1969), p. 23.
[15] H.R. Patch, *The Tradition of Boethius* (Oxford: Oxford University Press, 1935), p. 127 in Watts 1969: 13.

1190s, is modelled on Boethius's work.[16] Less well known to modern scholars than *The Consolation*, its combination of classical references and abundance of rhetorical devices and figures of speech ensured it remained a popular schoolbook throughout the late Middle Ages and Renaissance. The first two books consist of a lament on his recent fall from grace—he has recently been dismissed—and a diatribe against Fortune, personified as an old woman. He is visited by Phronesis who chides him for ignoring what he learnt in the past, consoles him in the penultimate book by reminding him of the importance of humility, and launches into a series of admonitions in the final book.[17] The work ends with the author dedicating his work to his previous employer, the Bishop of Florence, in a transparent bid to be given a second chance, buoyed by the soothing and encouraging words of Phronesis. He mentions his debt to a range of classical authors (Ovid, Lucan and Virgil), and frequently illustrates his comments with mythological parallels. The work is full of derivative wordplay, binary contrasts, and easily-memorized aphorisms, making it an ideal text for teaching:

> Sic gravius cadit hic quem format forma gigantis
> quam nanus cuius parvula forma sedet.
> Ut plumbum, gravius pluma paleaque lapillus,
> sic gravius cadit hic qui bona multa tulit. (I: 35-38)[18]

The way the second couplet mirrors the first, with the repetition of 'sic gravius cadit', the juxtaposition of 'format' and 'forma', and the con-

---

[16] There is no English translation available. A fourteenth-century Italian translation has been edited by Salvatore Battaglia (Turin: Unione Tipografico - Editrice Torinese, 1929). See Paul Gehl's *A Moral Art: Grammar, Society and Culture in Trecento Florence* (Ithaca-London: Cornell University Press, 1993), pp. 178-84, for a full English synopsis and an assessment of the significance of Settimello's text, and John Fleming's 'The Major Source of Bernat Metge's *Libre de Fortuna e Prudència*' in the *Journal of Hispanic Philology* 7 (Fall 1982), pp. 5-13.

[17] In Aristotelian theory, 'phronesis' is defined as a more practical form of analytical wisdom, in contrast to 'sophia' (and thus 'philosophy') which is related to an understanding of universal truths. This differentiation is not apparent in Settimello's depiction of Phronesis who is virtually indistinguishable in her moral standpoint from Boethius's Philosophy. Metge's choice of Prudence for his allegorical figure may be a translation of Settimello's Phronesis.

[18] 'So, he who has the build of a giant falls more heavily than the dwarf who is slightly built; lead falls more heavily than a feather, a stone more heavily than straw. Likewise he who has received many good things also falls more heavily.' See ll. 477-81 of the *Book of Fortune and Prudence* for Metge's adaptation of this excerpt.

trast between the alliterative 'plumbum' and 'pluma' illustrate some of Henry's stock-in-trade tools that helped keep his work in the classroom for centuries. It is during his formative years when he was learning Latin that Metge will have first encountered both *The Consolation* and the *Elegia*. As Fleming observes, the dialogue between the author-narrator and Fortune is direct in the *Elegia*, whereas it is mediated through Philosophy in *The Consolation*. Metge follows Settimello's lead here, not only in structural terms, but also in tone: the exchange with Fortune in both texts deteriorates into comically acrimonious name-calling. Note that the narrator in the *Book of Fortune and Prudence* shows little respect for Fortune from the outset, addressing her as 'woman' (*dona*), in contrast to the way he refers to Prudence as 'lady' (*senyora*).

Alan de Lille (c. 1116-1202) wrote his allegorical-philosophical epic, *Anticlaudianus* (or *The Good and Perfect Man*) between 1181 and 1184, just a decade before Settimello's *Elegia*.[19] Written in dactylic hexameters (epic metre), it consists of a prologue and nine books. Like Henry, Alan delights in wordplay. The narrative describes Nature's attempt to create the perfect man by enlisting the help of a host of other allegorical figures, including Concord, the Virtues, Reason, as well as Prudence and the Seven Liberal Arts. Towards the end of the work, Nobility wishes to contribute to the project but, as she herself has nothing to offer, she proposes consulting her mother, Fortune, who offers an array of gifts. Alan's description of Fortune's island home, and her physical appearance are reworked by Metge, in combination with the corresponding passage from the *Romance of the Rose*.

Judging by the number of surviving manuscripts (more than 250), and references to it in other works throughout Europe, the *Romance of the Rose* (*Roman de la Rose*) can justifiably be described as the most influential work of the French medieval period.[20] The original text, a complex courtly allegory of just over 4,000 lines, written by Guillaume de Lorris in the 1230s, was expanded fourfold with additional mate-

[19] The full title of the work is *Anticlaudianus de Antirufino*, which translates as 'The Opposite of Claudian's *Against Rufinus*'. Claudian's work was an invective against Rufinus, whom he considered a thoroughly evil man, hence the alternative English title of Alan's work, *The Good and Perfect Man*. The English translation by James Sheridan (Toronto: Pontifical Institute of Mediæval Studies, 1973) has a detailed and thorough introduction.

[20] There is an English translation by Frances Horgan (Oxford: Oxford University Press, 1994) and an excellent introductory study by Sarah Kay (London: Grant & Cutler, 1995).

rial—of a more philosophical rather than courtly character—by Jean
de Meun in about 1275. This change in tone is clear from the start of
Jean de Meun's contribution: it begins with a Boethian dialogue between the protagonist, the Lover, and the allegorical figure of Reason,
in which Reason cautions the Lover against elevating Fortune to the
status of goddess. She starts her argument with a description of Fortune's rocky island, her home, and her appearance. Jean de Meun
adapted and embellished the description in the *Anticlaudianus*; Metge
took material from both, and added a few touches of his own. So, for
example, in his description of the vegetation on the rocky island (ll.
230-39), he includes the cedar (in both source texts) as well as the
pine (an addition by Jean de Meun), omits the yew (as does Jean de
Meun), but adds the typically Mediterranean citron and kermes oak.
In the following passage (ll. 240-45), the nightingale is found in both
sources, but Metge follows Jean de Meun again in omitting the lark: instead he pairs the nightingale with the swallow (perhaps with reference to the myth of Philomena and Procne who were transformed into
those birds), and includes the cuckoo. However, the influence of the
Romance of the Rose on Metge's work goes beyond the few textual coin-
cidences in this passage. As Fleming points out, the *Romance*'s vernac-
ularization of the Latin tradition of philosophical-allegorical dialogue
that encompassed the works of Boethius and Alan de Lille set a prece-
dent, and provided the Catalan author with a conceptual model.

When writing the *Book of Fortune and Prudence*, Metge was undoubtedly influenced by, and borrowed from, works circulating at
court at that time. The four source texts mentioned so far provided
Metge with intellectual and textual models for the central part of the
work, the description of the island and the narrator's encounter with
Fortune and Prudence. However, the frame for this, in which he
emerges, troubled, from his Barcelona house at the outset, and then
returns there in the closing lines are not found in these works. Echoes
of two Catalan narrative poems by contemporaries—both of which fea-
ture in one of the manuscript witnesses of the *Book of Fortune*—are
found in the opening and closing sections of Metge's work. One is the
Adventure (*Ventura*), an allegorical narrative poem on courtly love by
Vicenç Comes, chamberlain to King Peter IV and King John I, and so
someone whom Metge would have known; the other is *The Tale* by
Guillem de Torroella, an Arthurian narrative in Catalan troubadouresque verse (but in which the characters' direct speech is in

French) written in the early 1370s.[21] It is an imagined continuation of the legend following the death of Arthur in which the author is transported from his native Mallorca to an Enchanted Isle (identified by some scholars as Sicily) where he finds King Arthur and his sister Morgana.

No time has elapsed between Bernat's pre-dawn stroll along the seafront and his return to Barcelona, still before daybreak: the entire narrative has taken place in the twinkling of an eye. There is a symmetrical circularity to the narrative, starting and ending in the same location, and consisting of two dialogues framed by a return journey. We are not certain exactly what is troubling the narrator at the outset, although given the economic climate it seems fair to surmise that it has at least a financial element to it. Certainly the motivation for this consolation is dissatisfaction with the transient nature of material wealth and its concomitant esteem. However, the narrator who returns to Barcelona seems little changed: calmer, perhaps, and more resigned, accepting that unless you have status you are worth nothing whatever Prudence—and the Church—may claim to the contrary. Just as no time has elapsed, so it would seem that there has been no great movement in the protagonist's outlook, as he returns to the very place he left at the start of the narrative.

This narrative frame, set in contemporary Barcelona, contrasts strikingly with the central fantastic and philosophical encounter with Fortune and Prudence. It illustrates the freedom with which Metge references more than one genre, and plays with the reader's expectations. The narrator's unfortunate predicament at the very outset is Boethian, but his subsequent trip in an unmanned rudderless vessel on 1 May—a date traditionally associated with love poetry—suggests a more romantic 'adventure' (*ventura*, ll. 7 and 158). The naked old man whom he encounters on the dockside is a liminal character, fulfilling a pivotal bridging role between the real Barcelona and the visionary island of Fortune and Prudence. Modern scholars have debated his identity in

---

[21] For Comes's role at the royal court, see Lluís Cabré's and Jaume Torró Torrent's 2010 article, 'Vicenç Comes, camérier royal, poète et ami de Bernat Metge', *Revue des Langues Romanes* 114, pp. 203-16. Neither poem has been translated into English, but both are available in modern editions: Gemma Brunat, ed., 2001, *Una ventura*, on the *Repertorio Informatizzato dell'Antica Letteratura Catalana* webpages (www.rialc.unina.it/43.1htm), and Anna Maria Compagna Perrone Capano, ed., *La faula per Guillem de Torroella* (Barcelona: Publicacions de l'Abadia de Montserrat - Edicions UIB, 2007).

much the same way, I suspect, as contemporary readers did.[22] Cabré's recent identification of him as the philosopher Diogenes who advocated poverty makes perfect sense. Metge does not name him explicitly to keep the readership guessing: is this a character from the real Barcelona world or one from the visionary component? Once he has been identified as Diogenes, however, the narrator's strongly-worded condemnation of him, repeated at the very end of the work when he returns to Barcelona, can be read as a rejection of his poverty-based ethos in a Barcelona where 'a man who does not make himself look important is valued less than a snail' (ll. 1186-87). The narrator, who we know from the outset has fallen on hard times, thus rushes home before the sun comes up to avoid being spotted in the street at such an inappropriately late hour.

The opening frame provides Metge with another device with which to confound his reader's expectations, and add layers of complexity to his argumentation. The ambiguity surrounding the narrator's identity—who is at one and the same time both the author and not the author—puts Metge himself at one remove from the narrative voice. It is this same technique that he uses with such aplomb some twenty years later in *The Dream*, enabling him to get away with espousing an almost heretically cynical stance with regard to the immortality of the soul. In the *Book of Fortune*, it allows us, for example, to see Fortune's questions about lending practices as a satirical comment on the contemporary financial crisis; to question the narrator's acceptance of Prudence's 'convincing' arguments; and to ponder just what it is the narrator (or Metge?) hopes we, his readers, will believe as he hurries 'back to my home, in the city of Barcelona, where I was born and where I will die, if I am to be believed' (ll. 1188-91): this story, or the arguments that Prudence suggests he uses to 'all those who doubt'?

---

[22] Some have suggested the character may be either Charon, the Underworld boatman, or Amyclas, whom Thomas Aquinas praises as an example of virtuous poverty in Dante's *Divine Comedy* (Paradise, Canto XI).

Translator's Note

In translating Metge's verse into English prose, I have tried to strike a balance between following the original closely enough for the translation to be of use for those seeking help when reading the Catalan, and at the same time providing a text that will give those unfamiliar with Catalan a readable and faithful rendering of Metge's original. I have chosen to Anglicise names, with the exception of those of Bernat Metge and his immediate family. I have used English equivalents for coinage mentioned in the text, with information about the original in the footnotes. Wherever possible, I have suggested additional reading in English for those who wish to learn more about the historical, social and literary background to the *Book of Fortune and Prudence*.

The translation is based on Lluís Cabré's 2010 edition of *Llibre de Fortuna i Prudència* (Barcelona: Barcino). I have also consulted Riquer's 1959 edition (*Obras de Bernat Metge*, Barcelona, Universitat de Barcelona, pp. 26-115), which includes a Castilian translation, and Lola Badia's and Xavier Lamuela's 1975 edition (*Obra completa de Bernat Metge*, Barcelona, Selecta, pp. 71-106). The English translation of quotations from Settimello's *Elegia* are my own.

In addition to the excellent support I have received from Joan Santanach at Barcino/Tamesis, I have been fortunate to benefit from the many helpful comments and suggestions that Barry Taylor (British Library) and Lluís Cabré (Universitat Autònoma de Barcelona) offered on drafts of both the introduction and the translation. Any remaining errors and shortcomings are all my own.

David Barnett
London, January 2011

BOOK OF FORTUNE AND PRUDENCE

JATS QUE EU SIA molt ocupats
d'alguns afers qui m'han portats
en tal perill d'on cuid morir,
4   ges per aisò no vull jaquir
en lo tinter ço que ausirets.
E si entendre hi volets
e notar la mia ventura,
8   coneixerets que pauca cura
deu hom haver del temporal;
car lo món és descominal,
que als uns dóna e als altres toll,
12   presant lo savi menys del foll
e l'hom cient menys del tapat;
e sempre sec la voluntat
los decebiments de Fortuna,
16   qui raisó no segueix alguna,
segons que per avant veirets.
E preg-vos que no us enugets
si prolixament la us recit,
20   ne si el dictat no és tan polit
com als llegidors se pertany.
E no us vullats traure susany
si no hi vesets rima subtil,
24   car ignorant sui de l'estil
dels trobadors del saber gai.

SAPJATS QUE EL primer jorn de mai,
l'any de la Nativitat santa
28   de Déu mil e tres-cents vuitanta
ez un de plus, ans d'alba clara,
quan m'haguí llavada la cara
ab aigua pura, e les mans,
32   al cor me véngron dolors grans
e tantost fui pus fred que gebre;
e tastí'm lo pols, e de febre
no em sentí punt, ans tenc la vena
36   son dret camí; mes hac tal pena
mon cor que no ho poria dir,
car semblava volgués eixir
l'arma del cors, tals surts donava.
40   E pensei-me que si m'anava

ALTHOUGH I AM much occupied with certain matters that have brought me such trouble that I fear for my life, I do not wish therefore to leave unwritten what you are about to hear.[1] And if you are prepared to pay attention and learn from my adventure, you will realise that one should not place much store by material goods, for the world is an unjust place where some have plenty and others are deprived, where the foolish are valued over the wise and the ignorant over the knowledgeable; and man's will is always subject to the schemes of Fortune, who is not governed by reason, as you will presently see. And I ask you not to become impatient if I draw out the telling of my adventure and if my writing is not as polished as my readers deserve. And please do not laugh at me if my verse lacks subtlety since I am afraid I am not practised in the Gay Science of the troubadours.[2]

BEFORE DAYBREAK on the first of May, in the year of our Lord 1381, after I had washed my face and hands in fresh water, I was struck by an acute pain in my heart and suddenly felt colder than frost; I checked my pulse, which was normal, and did not feel that I had a temperature, but I had a pain in my heart so severe that I cannot describe it: it was beating so fiercely, it seemed as if my soul were trying to break out of my body. So I thought that a short stroll by the sea might help to alleviate this

[1] The narrator's description of his perilous situation is a standard motif, a *lamentatio*, echoing the initial complaint against the vagaries of Fortune in two of Metge's main sources, Boethius's *The Consolation of Philosophy* and Henry of Settimello's *Elegia*. However, the 'matters' (Catalan *afers*) which Metge mentions may refer to a particular contemporary circumstance: a banking crisis in Barcelona, provoked by a broader economic depression, in the early 1380s.

[2] Troubadours composed lyric poetry in Provençal (also called Occitan or Langue d'Oc), and set it to music, during the twelfth and thirteenth centuries. Their art, known as the Gay Science (Catalan *saber gai*), enjoyed a revival in the fourteenth century: academies were established in Toulouse (1323) and Barcelona (1393), and competitions (*Jocs Florals*) were held to celebrate the work of the best poets. This verse form was highly appreciated in the royal court of the Crown of Aragon at the time Metge was writing. His apparent modesty is undoubtedly conventional.

un pauc deportar vers la mar,
pogra cella pena lleixar,
que si em duràs me corrompera.
44 E solet tenguí ma carrera
així com m'ho haguí pensat,
e encontinent fui delliurat
de la dolor qui em destrenyia.
48 Aprés un pauc viu que sesia
prop una barca un hom vell,
tot despullat, ab un capell
de cànem gros sobre son cap;
52 en l'una mà tenc un anap
e en l'altra un cantell de pa.
E quan me vi fortment cridà,
disent: «Sényer, mercè m'hajats!»
56 «En prom», dix eu, «què demandats?
Volets, per Dieu, algun diner?»
«No, sényer, que major mester
l'havets vós», dix ell, «que en cercats
60 e cascun jorn imaginats
com ne porets esser fornit;
ez ieu no trob major delit
sinó quan no hai què despendre,
64 car sui cert que no pot deixendre
lo meu estat en pus baix lloc;
e vós temets plus que gran foc
ço que deuríets desijar.
68 Mes preg-vos que em vullats donar
—e seré-us tostemps obligat—
un tabà que hai anit lleixat
en esta barca per oblit
72 (ab la qual arribei anit
en aicest lloc ab gran tempesta),
e donar-me-hets tota la resta
que possesesc en aquest món,
76 car, per ma fe, tan robat son
que no m'hi poria llevar.»
«En prom», dix ieu, «segons que em par,
de pauc vos tenits per pagat.
80 Volgra m'haguéssets asemprat
que us donàs la roba que port.»
Car ieu era de tal acord

agony, because if it continued so, my health would surely deteriorate further. And so I headed off on my own for my stroll as I had planned, and straight away I was released from the pain that had been distressing me. After a short while, I saw an old man sitting near a boat, completely naked, with a hat of coarse hemp on his head; he held a cup in one hand and a piece of bread in the other.[3] And when he saw me, he shouted:

"Sir, have mercy on me!"

"My good man," I said, "what is it you are asking for? Are you begging for money?"

"No, sir," he said, "for you need that more than I do; you're the one who's always looking for it and every day imagines how he can lay his hands on it. Whereas I'm never happier than when I've nothing to spend, because then I know for sure that I cannot sink any lower; yet you are more frightened of what you should in fact desire than you are of a great fire.[4] However, I would like you to fetch me—and I will be forever obliged to you—a cape that I left on this boat which brought me here last night during a great storm. In doing so you will be giving me all that remains of my worldly possessions. I'm afraid I'm not suitably dressed to go and get it for myself."

"My good man," I said, "it seems to me that you're asking for very little. I would rather you had asked me for the shirt off my back." Be-

---

[3] The old man's lack of attire, the fact that he is holding a cup, and his caustic philosophical exchange in which he extols the merits of poverty, identify him as the Greek philosopher Diogenes the Cynic (c. 412-323 BC), an appropriate figure to set the narrator off on his philosophical adventure.

[4] In other words, he fears poverty (what he should desire) more than being burnt.

que la'm despullàs mantinent.
84   E pugé-me'n alegrement
alt en la barca, ses dir àls.
Ez ell, com a vilanàs fals,
com haguí l'esquena girada,
88   tantost hac la barca varada
ab me, qui fui dins tot solet.
De vela e de rems fui net,
e de govern, car no n'hi hac.
92   «No em son cobert d'aquest escac»,
dix ieu, «per què el joc n'és perdut.
Ab falses tretes m'ha vençut
aquest traidor ab qui em fiava;
96   mes jo la li faré pus blava,
en ma fe, si jamés lo vei.»
Veu's qui a vil hom fa servei
com ne cobra mal gasardó!
100   «D'aquestes burles hajam pro»,
dix ieu, «e puis vendrà la guerra.»
E volguí-me'n eixir en terra,
mes no en viu en neguna part.
104   «Ai las!», dix ieu, «Ara sui fart
de ben servir, pus mal me'n pren!
Ai las! E què em val si refrèn
de lleigs vicis ma voluntat?
108   Ai las! Per què val pietat
si, havent-la, consella hom mal?
Ai las! E per què sent egual
de l'home just lo pecador?
112   Eras veig que és en gran error
lo món. E ja s'hi tingués foc!
Car ja ven lo mortal estoc
qui em vol l'arma del cors llunyar.»
116   Aprés un pauc va refrescar
la mar e el vent e el temps sinestre,
que semblava que fos pinestre
la barca, o sac esquinçat,
120   car l'aigua qui per un forat
entrava per l'altre eixia;
e puis la barca qui prenia
tals surts que semblava volàs.
124   «Cest viatge serà ivaç

cause I was ready to strip and give him my clothes then and there. And so I gladly boarded the boat without another word. Meanwhile the old man, like the double-crossing villain he was, as soon as I had turned my back, pushed the boat off with only me on board, and no sails, oars, or rudder.

"I hadn't prepared myself for a move like that," I said, "and I've been caught out. This traitor has got the better of me with his crafty tricks, but I'll pay him back with interest, I can assure you, if I ever set eyes on him again." You see what a poor reward you get for helping out a villain. "Enough of this fooling around," I said, "I shall do battle with him at a later date." I was keen to be back on dry land, but there was no sight of it anywhere.

"Alas!" I said, "I've had enough of doing people favours—they just miscarry! Alas! What good does it do me if I make an effort to refrain from ugly vices? Alas! What's the use of compassion if, when you show it, you discover you're poorly advised? Why does the sinner feel the same as the just man? I see now that there is something seriously awry in the world. I wish the whole lot would go up in flames! Because the deadly blow that is going to part my soul from my body is already on its way."

After a while the sea became choppier, the wind picked up, and the weather took a turn for the worse. The boat felt like a wicker basket or a ripped bag, because the water that came in through one hole poured out through another, and it was tossed so high that it seemed to be flying.

"From the look of things," I said, "this trip is soon going to be over."

finit», dix ieu, «segons que em par.»
Pógrets-me lladoncs descalçar
de rialles, que no ho sentira;
128   car, cert, no crei que nulla vira
pogués volar pus prestament.
Aprés un pauc cessà lo vent
e l'alba començà lusir,
132   e regardei entorn e engir
de me, si pogra veser terra;
e semblà'm que a la part esquerra,
entorn vint milles lluny de mi,
136   terra vesés, e no em sabí
de gaug què m'hac esdevengut;
e el mal que havia sostengut
me sovenc menys que quan nasquí.
140   Perquè és ver que aprés gran camí
plau a l'home cansat repòs;
ez aprés gran secada, ros;
ez aprés nuit, lo dia clar;
144   ez aprés gran fam, bon menjar;
ez aprés marriment, trop riure.
«Encara», dix ieu, «poré viure
e fer esmena de mos torts
148   e dar almoines per los morts
preiant Déu que els do paradís.»
E la barca, susau e llis,
mentre ieu era en est pensament,
152   acostec-me en un pauc moment
prop una roca fort agresta;
e tantost, ses altra requesta,
de la barca salté al ferm.
156   «Encara», dix ieu, «no em referm
que sia de mort delliurat,
car ma ventura m'ha portat
en lloc on de fam moriré;
160   e puis, que jamés no seré
en cimenteri sebollit,
car no serà mon cors poirit
que feres l'hauran devorat.
164   Car no conec que hi haja estat
home vivent, ne hic haurà
aitant com lo món durarà,

At that time, you could have removed my shoes for a joke without me even noticing; because in truth I do not believe that an arrow could have flown faster than that boat. After a short while the wind dropped, the sun started to rise, and I looked all around me to see if I could catch sight of any land. And it seemed to me that about twenty miles off to my left I could spy land, and I felt overwhelmed with joy. The hardship that I had endured suddenly seemed as distant as the pain I felt in being born. It is surely true that rest is especially welcome to a tired man after a long journey, as is dew after a severe drought, the clear light of day after night, good food after great hunger, and hearty laughter after sadness.

"I can yet live on," I said, "put right what I have done wrong, and give alms for the dead, praying God that he may grant them Paradise."

And in the short while I was absorbed in this thought, the boat smoothly and evenly transported me to a most inhospitable rock. Without any further ado, I leapt from the boat on to *terra firma*.

"I'm still not yet able to confirm," I said, "that I've managed to escape death, because my adventure has brought me to a place where I shall surely die of hunger. What is more, I shall never be buried in a churchyard because wild beasts will devour my corpse before it has had the chance to decompose. I do not know if man has ever lived here, or car lloc ho vei deshabitat.»

168 Eras dic que és bé veritat
que no sap hom què s'hic desig;
car cascun jorn haurets fastig
d'aisò d'on gaug esperarets,
172 ez haurets plaers mantes vets
d'aisò d'on esperats tristor.
E per ço que major dolor
hajats de la perplexitat
176 en què ieu era lladoncs pausat,
dir-vos-he, com pus breu porai,
lo lloc quin era ne l'esmai
que n'hac tan fort lo meu trist cor,
180 que em meravell com prest no mor
cascuna veu quan li recorda;
e no hai ges pasor que em morda
algun, provant-me lo contrari,
184 si doncs ab document falsari
son injust procés no fundava.

LA MAR SAPJATS que environava
la roca de cascuna part,
188 que era tan alta que ab un dard
tocara hom al cel primer.
E quan lo vent era lleuger
e el temps adonós e temprat,
192 la mar estava en son estat,
que null enuig ne dan fasia
en aicell lloc, e puis floria
cascuna planta en tots temps.
196 Fulles e flors e fruits ensems
hi havia mentre durava
lo temps susau, mes co·s mudava
no hi calia mais confessar;
200 car la mar vesérets alçar
tan alt que la roca cobria,
ez aprés pauc temps deixendia
fins als abís, e puis tornava
204 en cell estat ez arrencava
totes les plantes d'aquell lloc,
les flors e els fruits—semblava foc
los hagués blasits—e les fulles,

ever could until the end of the world because as far as I can see this place is completely uninhabited."

I tell you it is true that man does not know what he desires. With each passing day you will tire of what you thought you were going to enjoy, and on many occasions you will find pleasing what you thought was going to bring you sadness. And so that you can best understand just how perplexed I felt at that time, I must describe for you—in as few words as possible—what that place was like and the dreadful sinking feeling that I felt in my sorry heart.[5] It is a wonder I do not drop down dead every time I recall it. And I am not in the least concerned that someone is going to sue me by proving it to be otherwise, unless their case is based on false documentation.

THE ROCK WAS surrounded by the sea on all sides and rose so high that you could reach the First Heaven with an arrow.[6] When the wind was light and the weather pleasant and temperate, the sea remained calm and caused no trouble or damage on the island, and all the plants were always in bloom. Leaves, flowers, and fruits all appeared together as long as the mild weather lasted. But when it changed, all you could do was make your confession because you saw the sea rise up so high that it covered the rock and then soon after plunge down to the abyss before rising up again. It wrecked all the plants there, the flowers, the fruit—which looked as if it had been scorched by fire—and the leaves,

---

[5] Metge's subsequent description of the island draws extensively on a lengthy passage from Alan de Lille's *Anticlaudianus* in which Nobility goes in search of her mother Fortune (VII.405-VIII.47), and Reason's warning against Fortune in the *Romance of the Rose* (vv. 5891-5916).

[6] According to medieval cosmology, the heavens were divided into seven spheres, the first of which was known as the Lunar Heaven.

208 ensems ab trestotes les brulles,
car una no n'hi romania.
Ez aprés un pauc revenia
lo bon temps e cessava el mal;
212 e fasia puis atrestal
lo bon temps, quan lo mal venia.
Al pus alt d'aicest lloc havia
un gran boscatge tot plantat
216 d'arbres diversos e regat
en algús llocs e en altres no.
E tantost fui d'opinió
que no hi era Déu ni natura,
220 car no hi hac orde ne mesura
ne res qui fos fait per raisó.
La major part dels arbres fo
de fruit e fulles despullada,
224 e l'altra part era ornada
de fruits e de vestiments rics.
E els arbres que eren pus antics
e de pus alta noiridura
228 havien menor estatura
que cells que eren de baix llinatge.
E contenien de paratge
lo cedre ab lo poncemer,
232 e lo gran pi ab lo murter,
e l'arbre blanc ab lo coscoll;
e el sàlzer no es veia sadoll
de llevar fruit; e lo perer
236 no en lleva ges, ne lo pomer;
e l'oliver era tot sec,
e lo presseguer null entec
rebia per calor del sol.
240 En aicest lloc lo rossinyol
no cantava, ne l'oreneta,
mes lo cogull, qui ab veu neta
cantava lais, així com sol,
244 e la cigala ab lo mussol,
qui li tenien contracant;
e fasien so discordant
li ausel qui el solen far plasent.
248 D'est lloc prenien naiximent
dos rius contraris en color,

together with all the buds, so that not a single one remained. And then shortly afterwards, the good weather returned and the bad subsided. And the good weather repeated this pattern every time the bad weather struck.[7]

At the highest point on the island there was a large grove, planted with all variety of different trees, some parts of which were fed by a river and others not. And I was suddenly struck that neither God nor nature was present there, because there was no order or balance, or anything governed by reason. More than half of the trees were stripped of leaves and fruit, and the rest were decorated with fruits and rich adornments. The oldest and most venerable trees were shorter than those of poor lineage. And they vied with each other in nobility, the cedar with the citron, the tall pine with the myrtle, and the poplar with the kermes oak. The willow never tired of bearing fruit, but neither the pear tree nor the apple tree produced any. The olive tree was completely dry and the peach tree did not succumb to any disease when subjected to direct sunlight.[8] And the nightingale did not sing there, nor did the swallow, but the cuckoo sang lays in a clear voice, as is its custom, and the cicada and little owl accompanied him with counter melodies.[9] And birds which usually sing melodiously made a discordant sound.

Two rivers rose from their source there. They were complete op-

[7] Literally, 'the good weather then did the same when the bad weather came' meaning that the good and bad weather changed frequently and abruptly.

[8] Selecting typically Mediterranean species from his sources—and discarding others—Metge describes the island as the opposite of a *locus amoenus* (literally a 'pleasant place', a literary term used to denote an idyllic setting, often a garden), where the natural order of things is turned on its head. The fruit of the evergreen citron tree (*Citrus medica*) was valued in medieval times for its medicinal rather than culinary properties. The kermes oak (*Quercus coccifera*) is an evergreen shrub, native to the Mediterranean.

[9] The swallow, cuckoo, and cicada are local species that Metge himself has incorporated into his reworking of the source material. The little owl (*Athene noctua*) is partially diurnal and has a strident call. Note the reference to art forms popular at the Catalan-Aragonese court: lays, lyric poems sung by French troubadours, and polyphony ('counter melodies', Catalan *contracant*), increasingly used in secular music, and closely associated in the fourteenth century with Guillaume de Machaut (c. 1300-77), the author of *Remède de Fortune* (see note 21).

en llur moviment e en sabor,
cascun d'ells havent sa natura.

252   Car cell qui havia la figura
e la sabor pus agradable,
ab l'apetit insaciable,
aprés que un pauc n'haguí tastat,

256   lo meu cors hac hidropicat
e portat a perill de mort,
car lo beure em donà pus fort
ardor e set quant mais bevia;

260   e puis, que partir no podia
los ulls de mirar tan bell riu.
L'altre no era tan joliu
ne de sabor tan graciosa,

264   abans era pus amargosa
que si mesclada fos ab fel;
semblava que ab les nuus del cel
hagués desig de batallar,

268   car [ieu] no pogra divisar
ne figurar son pujament;
e puis deixendia corrent
ab gran brogit e fort horrible.

272   Dir-vos-he cosa incredible:
a me covenc beure d'est flum,
no contrastant que n'isqués fum
de sofre quan és sobre el foc,

276   car no podia trobar lloc
on guarís de la malaltia,
e puis la set qui em destrenyia
volent-me tolre l'apetit.

280   E de continent fui guarit
pus haguí d'aquest riu begut;
lo qual, pus m'hac dada salut,
ab l'altre riu fec companyia.

284   E tengueren tots una via
vivent abdosos de comú,
mes lo naiximent de cascú
era divers e separat.

288   Quan tot açò haguí mirat
pugí-me'n alt en una roca,
qui em pens que ab una empenta poca
la gitara hom dins la mar,

posites in colour, movement, and taste, each with its own nature. Within a short while of drinking—with insatiable thirst—from the one that looked and tasted more agreeable, my body was afflicted with dropsy and in mortal danger. The more I drank, the more intense the burning sensation and the sharper my thirst, and yet I could not take my eyes off it, such a beautiful river it was. The other one was not as pretty, nor did it have as pleasant a taste, but tasted more bitter than if it had been mixed with bile. It seemed to want to do battle with the clouds in the sky, because I could not discern or imagine from what height it flowed and then cascaded down with a loud and most terrifying din. I must now tell you something incredible: I had to drink from this river, even though it was giving off fumes like burning sulphur, because I could not find a place to cure myself of my affliction and furthermore my thirst was driving me to drink there so that it might be quenched. As soon as I had drunk from that river, I was immediately cured. And once it had restored my health, it joined the other river, and both followed a single course together, yet the source of each one was different and separate.[10]

When I had seen all this, I climbed up high onto a rocky outcrop which I think could have been knocked into the sea with just one lit-

[10] In the description of the two rivers, Metge again combines elements from his two main sources for the passage (*Anticlaudianus* VII.439-478 and the *Romance of the Rose* vv. 5948-6039). He does, however, introduce his own material: for example, in his version it is the narrator who drinks from the rivers, rather than anonymous impersonal characters ('cil qui ... bevant', 'those who drink', v. 5960), and Metge uses the thirst-inducing properties of the first to provide the justification for drinking from the less visually appetizing second one.

292   car los fonaments viu llunyar
del firmament ultra mesura,
ez eren plens de corcadura
e crivellats com a garbell.
296   Al mig havia un castell
de cascuna part ben murat.
A l'una part era daurat
ez encastat de peires fines,
300   ab veirieres crestal·lines
historiades subtilment;
e puis, que era el seu païment
tan clar, tan llis com un mirall,
304   e no semblava cop de mall
en aicest lloc hagués ferit,
car no pogra esser pus polit
qui n'hagués passat brunidor.
308   De l'altra part, saul vostra honor,
no hi pógrets veser mais sutzura,
tan horrible que ab escriptura
no la us poria declarar,
312   car no em pens faça a comparar
al plus sutze lloc que hajats vist.
Mon cor fo lladoncs molt pus trist
e tenguí'm per dit que mort era,
316   car viu denant mi la pus fera
domna que mai ausíssets dir.
E si no us enujats d'ausir
com era gint afaiçonada
320   e de bells vestits arresada,
jo us ho diré ab fort grossers mots.

PRIMERAMENT los cabells tots
tenc escampats sobre la cara,
324   e la part detràs fon pus clara
e menys pelosa que cristall.
L'un ull semblava fos gra d'all,
ben parat, e no se'n vesia,
328   del qual un riuellet eixia
qui demostrava que ploràs;
l'altre movia gran solaç,
que sinó riure no fasia,
332   e movia tal alegria

tle push: I saw its foundations crumbling downwards at an alarming rate, and they were full of woodworm, and riddled with holes like a sieve.[11] In the middle of this rock was a castle, well fortified throughout. On one side, it was golden, encrusted with precious stones, and had subtly decorated stained glass windows. The paving on the floors was as clear and smooth as a mirror: it looked as if no hammer blow had ever struck this place because it could not have been shinier if someone had polished it. On the other side of the castle, you could see—and begging your pardon—nothing but filth, so repulsive that I could not describe it to you in writing because I believe it is beyond compare with even the filthiest place you have ever seen.

My heart then sank even further, and I could have sworn that I was dead, because I saw before me the ugliest woman that you could ever hear speak of. And if you do not mind hearing how elegantly turned out she was, and what beautiful garments she was wearing, I will tell you in very crude terms.

FIRST OF ALL, her hair completely covered her face, and the back of her head was as clear and hairless as glass. She had one eye that looked like a clove of garlic, did not move, and through which she could not see; the little trickle of tears that issued from it showed that she was weeping. The other eye was a source of great solace, so much so that she could not help but laugh, and it expressed such joy that she

[11] Metge continues to select and combine elements from the *Anticlaudianus* (VIII.1-12) and the *Romance of the Rose* (vv. 6049-6084) for his description of Fortune's castle.

que semblava fos embriaga.
En la faç hac una tal plaga
que la meitat era mig morta.
336 E fon cinta d'una redorta
de vímens mesclats ab fil d'aur.
Los seus vestits trop gran tresaur
mostraven que devia haver,
340 jats que hom podia ben veser
que no eren tals prop la carn.
En ma fe, no ho dic per escarn
ne com no m'altava molt d'ella:
344 no em pens que en la sua gonella
cabessen dos diners de pebre.
Crei que ella em cuidava decebre
metent-me garsa per colom,
348 car no dava parvén que un plom
presàs tot quant ella vesia,
que dels continents que fasia
no en pogra far mais l'emperaire.
352 Però no us pensets que fos gaire
sencera ne forts de son cors,
que un gep portava sobre el dors,
e puis, que era llejament ranca,
356 car del taló se dava en l'anca
de l'una part quan se movia,
e com avant anar volia
tornava dos passos atràs;
360 e puis havia la un braç
pus curt que l'altre la meitat.
E quan haguí un pauc mirat
aquest diable tan horrible,
364 que ab moviment incomprensible
una gran roda que menava
de l'una mà en l'altra mudava
incessantment, ab gran brogit,
368 e[u] volguí tornar un petit
atràs, e no em poguí ges moure.
Lladoncs me pogra tot hom noure
qui em volgués mal, que no em tornara;
372 e pausei en terra la cara
mais per pasor que per vergonya.

seemed drunk. She had such a sore on her face that one side of it was half dead. She was wearing a belt of wicker entwined with gold thread. Her garments suggested that great treasure lay beneath, but you could clearly see that this was not the case. Take my word for it, I am not saying this in mockery or because I did not like her: but I do not think that her gown could hold tuppence worth of pepper.[12] I think that she was trying to trick me by offering me a pig in a poke[13] because she did not care a straw for anything that she saw; she put on more airs and graces than an emperor. But do not imagine that her body was either healthy or strong: she had a hump on her back, and what is more, she was grotesquely lame so that she kicked one of her buttocks with her heel every time she moved, and when she wanted to step forward she ended up taking two paces backwards. One of her arms was half as short as the other.

And when I had looked on this diabolical creature for a short while, as she continuously tossed a large wheel from one hand to the other with an incomprehensible movement and terrible din, I wanted to step back a little, but found I could barely move. Then, anyone who wished me ill could have done me harm, and would have met with little resistance. I lay face down on the ground, more from fear than from shame.

---

[12] The gown (Catalan *gonella*) was worn over an undershirt, but under the outer garments. The precise meaning of this observation is unclear. Metge is contrasting Fortune's expensive-looking outer garments with her undergarments: the observation that it 'could not hold tuppence worth of pepper' (Catalan *no [...] cabessen dos diners de pebre*) may suggest that the garment was ill-fitting or perhaps riddled with holes (note that in the fourteenth century, many spices, pepper among them, were an expensive luxury). The description of Fortune's clothing in the *Romance of the Rose* as being perfumed and dyed with 'les herbes et les graines' ('plants and seeds', v. 6098) may have been the inspiration: perhaps Metge is suggesting that her clothing is poorly perfumed?

[13] Literally, 'giving me a heron for a dove' (Catalan *metent-me garsa per colom*).

«LLEVATS-VOS, AMIC, de la ronya»,
dix ella, «e no us esperdats
376 per res que vejats ne ojats,
car ieu sui cella que en pauc temps
pusc los mesquins llevar dels fems
e els grans senyors gitar en terra.»
380 E, prenent-me pel braç esquerre,
féu-me llevar encontinent.
Ez ieu preguei-la humilment,
gitant-me tot en la carrera,
384 que em degués dir son nom qual era,
car ja m'era cert son poder.
«Amic, pus que volets saber
mon nom qual és, sapjats de cert
388 (e preg-vos que ho tingats cobert,
que no ho sapja persona alguna)
lo meu propi nom és Fortuna,
qui don bé e mal a qui em vull.
392 Mes ges per aisò no em despull
de res que don, car bé ho sé tolre
quan ieu me vull, e faç absolre
de tots crims molts hòmens malvats.
396 E si els justs vesets condemnats
a les vets, no us meravellets,
car ieu ho faç. Ara sabets
qual és mon nom ne per què em plau
400 sia secret: car l'hom qui cau
de son estat podets pensar
que fa son poder de tornar
al primer punt, e si sabia
404 que ieu ho fasés, no em presaria
un all ni quant li pogués dar;
e quan no ho sap, faç-li rodar
lo cap, e baralla's ab Déu
408 com no li torna ço del seu
o no li dóna en breu la mort.»
«Dona», dix ieu, «a mi plau fort
tot ço que m'havets recitat,
412 car vei que de l'adversitat
que sofir, vós n'havets la colpa.»
«Fols és», dix ella, «qui m'encolpa,
ne qui de mos faits parla mal.

"PICK YOURSELF UP, my friend, off the dirt," she said, "and don't let anything you see or hear unhinge you, because I am the one who in the blink of an eye can raise the wretched from the sewers and bring noble lords crashing down to earth." And she took hold of my left arm and straight away lifted me up. Prostrating myself before her on the path, I humbly asked her to tell me her name, as I was already convinced of her power.

"Friend, as you want to know my name, know for certain (and I beg you to keep this under cover so that no one finds out) that my name is Fortune, and I dispense good and bad to whomever I like. But I do not relinquish my rights to anything that I give out: I know full well how to take it away again when I want to, and I ensure that many wicked men are absolved of all their crimes. And if on occasion you see the just condemned, do not be amazed because it is my handiwork. Now you know what my name is and why I like to keep it secret: a man who loses his status is, as you can imagine, going to do everything he can to regain his former position. If he knew that I was behind his fall he wouldn't give a fig about me or about what I could give him. And when he doesn't know, I put his head in a spin, and then he starts quarrelling with God for not giving him back what is his, or for not granting him a speedy death."

"Woman," I said, "I'm very pleased about everything you've told me because I now see that you are to blame for the dreadful situation I'm in."

"Whoever puts the blame on me," she said, "is a fool, as is anyone who criticises what I do. If I am not as generous with you as you'd like,

416   E si no us son tan liberal
com desijats, quin tort prenets?
Parlats gallard, car bé saubets
que gint parlar amics gasanya.»

420   «DONA», DIX EU, «fort sots estranya.
E pus fets mal, no us ho diré?
Per vostre dit vos provaré
que nulla fermetat havets:
424   car ço que dats despuis tolets,
e fets rics cells qui no ho mereixen;
e puis, cells qui ab Déu s'ireixen
fets pujar pus alt que els humils;
428   e fets deixendre los subtils
e pujar alt hòmens grossers;
e fets de tacanys cavallers
e papes d'hòmens reprovats;
432   e, finalment, així n'usats
de femater fins al sant paire.
Temps fo que us tenia per maire,
mes ara vei que em sots madrastra;
436   temps fo que em seguien per rastre
molts escuders: ara no em volen;
temps fo que cells qui ara volen
sobre les nus eren jus mi;
440   temps fon que tants plasers haguí
com pogués haver hom del món;
temps fon que tots aquells qui són
grans mestres eren mos amics,
444   mes ara em giten grans p[r]esics
quan me vesen jaure al baix
e giten-me cascú son llaix,
bascant e cridant temps passat,
448   e dien: "Veu's qui ha gastat
per sa gran colpa ço del seu"!
E sap bé Nostre Senyor Déu
que d'açò vós n'havets lo tort.
452   Al bon hom pits li és que mort
quan sa fama perd, majorment
quan veu que no és malmirent
d'açò d'on hom l'haurà blasmat.
456   E las! Dolça prosperitat,

how does that harm you? Speak boldly, because you well know that courteous words win friends."

"WOMAN," I SAID, "you are most odd. If you're doing bad things, why shouldn't I say so? It's clear to me from what you've just said that you lack consistency. What you give you then take away; you make those who don't deserve it wealthy; you elevate those who quarrel with God above those who show humility; you demote the bright and promote the stupid; you turn misers into knights and reprobates into popes; and, finally, you treat everyone equally, from the dung-shoveller to the Holy Father. Once upon a time I thought of you as a mother, but now I see that you are more of a stepmother. Once I was followed by a whole coterie of squires; now they're not interested. There was a time when those who fly above the clouds were below me; when I enjoyed as many pleasures as a man could have in the world. I was once friends with all those who are considered great teachers, but now they lecture me when they see how far I have fallen. They insult me, reproach me, and remind me of the past, saying: 'Look who's wasted everything he ever had through no fault but his own!' And Our Lord God well knows that all this is your doing.

"For a good man, the loss of his reputation is a fate worse than death, especially when he sees that the accusations against him are un-

on est ne per què em vas fugent?
Convertit has mon jausiment
en greu dolor, d'on cuid morir.
460   Lo major dol que hom pot sofrir
és, a mon jui, haver usat
d'honor e de felicitat
e que hom se'n veja puis desert.
464   En l'una mà tenits cobert
molt verí, e en l'altra triaga;
en l'una mà vei que s'amaga
molt fel, e en l'altra gran dolçor;
468   en l'una mà plasent odor
tenits, e en l'altra molt pudent.
Per què no dau primerament
del mal, puis que donets del bé?
472   No sabets ab quin plaser ve
salut aprés l'enfermetat?
Sí es fa aprés l'adversitat
lo bé, mes no pas lo contrari.
476   Vós, quan fait havets l'hom clavari
de molt aur, prenets-li la clau.
¿E no sabets que pus lleig cau
un gran gigant que un petit nan,
480   e plom que palla, e fust gran
ne dóna major colp que el poc?
No us cuidets que ho diga per joc,
car no he desig de burlar.
484   Tot açò puix testificar,
per tal com de tot he tastat.
Sapjats que ieu hai per espatxat
que, despuis que la nostra maire
488   fec pecar nostre primer paire,
no ha nascut hom en est món
qui tan greus mals com en mi són
haja sofert, Déu me n'ajud.
492   Ai las! Pus així son perdut,
per què sots tan descominal
que no em lleixats sofrir mon mal
en lloc on no fos conegut?
496   Més amaria esser batut
ab vergues de bou en Bolunya,
denant tuit, que si en Catalunya

founded.[14] Alas! Sweet prosperity, where are you and why do you desert me? You have turned my pleasure into great pain which I fear will be my death. The worst grief that can befall a man to my mind is to have tasted honour and happiness and then to be deprived of them. In one hand you have concealed a large dose of poison, and in the other the antidote; in one hand I can see bile aplenty is hidden, and in the other great sweetness; one hand has a fragrant smell, the other stinks. Why don't you dole out the bad before the good? Don't you know how great a return to good health feels after an illness, as when good times follow adversity? But it doesn't work the other way round. First you make a man the custodian of a hoard of gold, and then you take away the key. Don't you know that a tall giant falls more heavily than a short dwarf, like lead compared to straw, and that a plank of wood strikes a heftier blow than a twig? Don't suppose that I'm saying this for fun: I'm in no mood for jokes. I can testify to all this because I have experienced it myself. I'm sure that ever since our mother led our first father to sin,[15] there has not been a man in this world who has suffered such ills as I have, may God help me. Alas! As I am so utterly lost, why are you being so cruel that you won't let me suffer my misfortune somewhere where I'm not known? I'd rather be beaten with bullwhips in Bologna, in full

[14] The following section in which the narrator bemoans his current misfortunes and rails against Fortune is based on the first book of Henry of Settimello's *Elegia*.

[15] In other words, since Eve persuaded Adam to eat the apple from the Tree of Knowledge.

un pèl de mon cap arrencaven.
500 Ai las! De tots cells qui m'honraven
he gran desig esser semblant,
e cadascú ha pasor gran
de veure's en lo meu partit.
504 Quan me vesien ben vestit,
cells qui es fasien mos amics
disien que ells eren antics
servidors de tot mon llinatge;
508 mes ara em giten a carnatge
quan vesen que no els puix res dar.
Ab res no pot hom tant provar
cascun amic com en mal temps,
512 car lo vertader volrà ensems
morir ab vós en tota part.
L'altre us dirà: "De mal son fart,
per què m'haurets a perdonar."
516 Sabets què em fa desesperar?
Mantes vets, quan sui en mon llit,
jo cuidara dormir la nit
e no puix ges los ulls tancar,
520 e per força em cové girar
de les vegades més de cent;
e per pauc que estiga dorment
no somiu àls mes vanitats
524 e que sofir adversitats
pijors que celles qui em devoren,
les quals tots cells qui Déu adoren
no porien imaginar
528 ne escriure, posat que la mar
fos tinta e lo cel paper.
Maleit sia cell qui primer
de terra em llevà quan fui nat!
532 Maleit sia el vilà orat
qui em batejà, com no em matà!
Maleit sia qui m'enconà,
com no m'hi mesclà rialgar!
536 Car més val dejús terra estar
que quan hom sofer pits de mort.
Digats, dona, de què us tinc tort?
Digats, mala mort vos hic lleu!,

view of everyone, than have a single hair pulled from my head in Catalonia.[16] Alas! I want to be on an equal footing with all those who used
to honour me, yet now they are all terrified of finding themselves in my
shoes. When those who pretended to be my friends saw me smartly
dressed, they claimed that they had long been in my family's service;
but now they drop me, unceremoniously, when they see that there is
nothing I can do for them. There's no better test of friendship than a
spot of misfortune, because a true friend will always want to die with
you, no matter what. And the other will say to you: 'You'll have to forgive me, but I've had enough of misfortune, thanks.' Do you know what
makes me despair? Many times, when I'm lying in bed at night, I try to
sleep but I can hardly close my eyes; instead, I end up tossing and turning more than a hundred times over, and then, shortly after I do get to
sleep, I dream of nothing but vanities, that I am suffering even greater
adversities than the ones that are eating me up, that no Christian could
either imagine or describe, even if the sea were turned to ink and the
sky to paper. A curse on the one who first picked me up off the ground
after I was born! A curse on the mad old man who baptised me, for
not killing me! A curse on the one who first gave me pap, for not mix-
ing it with poison! It's better to be six feet under than to suffer a fate
worse than death. Tell me, woman, what have I ever done to harm you?

[16] Compare the corresponding text from Metge's source, Settimello's *Elegia*: 'It is
sweeter for the wretched to live in a foreign land than in their own, where every one of
their disgraces is well known. I prefer my own dishonour to be known to the distant In-
dians than to those whom this place has made my neighbours' ('Dulcius est miseris
aliena vivere terra / quam propria, male qua singula probra patent. / Malo meum sciri
longinquis dedecus Indis / quam quos vicinos efficit ipse locus'; *Elegia* I.111-114). In the
Book of Fortune and Prudence, the distant lands are not the Indies but Bologna, the city
where Settimello had studied. The alliteration is in the original Catalan (*batut / ab vergues de bou en Bolunya*).

540 fiu-vos jamés causa tan greu
que tal pena deja passar?»

«BÈSTIA SOTS, segons que em par»,
dix ella, «perquè em deshonrats
544 e sens tota raisó us clamats:
no hi ha bon guardó al servei.
No us recorda, segons que vei,
que quan en aquest món vingués
548 res no hic portàs, e puis hagués
menjar e beure e vestir
e diners, e no podets dir
que per mi no n'hajats hagut:
552 tant vos n'he dat com m'ha plagut;
ara no us en vull pus donar.
Sabets quan vos pógrets clamar?
Si més que us he dat vos tolgués.
556 Recorda-us quants plasers hagués
en temps de la prosperitat?
Pagats-me ço que us he prestat
e siam amics com dabans.
560 E no sabets que els senyors grans
e els homes simples tinc al puny,
e faç-los refredar al juny
e sofrir calor a Nadal?
564 Als uns don bé e als altres mal,
e faç tornar los jóvens vells.
Digats, què us par dels mogobells?
Han pres, a vostre jui, bell tomb?
568 [Car] l'aur han convertit en plom
los canviadors que sabets,
e si els deits: "Senyors, què em devets?",
respondran-vos que bona amor.
572 No els fan ara tan gran honor
les gents com al bon temps fasien,
quan lo mercuri convertien
en aur de vint-i-tres quirats.
576 Tals se tendrien per pagats
que hi perdessen vui la meitat
—pus no hi ha fe ne veritat—,
que no es tengueren per contents
580 que de vint sous fessen cinc-cents

Tell me—and may you die a horrible death!—did I ever do such a terrible thing to you that I should have to endure such tribulation as this?"

"YOU'RE AN IDIOT, I find," she said, "because you dishonour me and you complain without good reason that there is no reward for service. As far as I can see, you do not remember that when you came into this world, you did not bring anything with you, but then you had food, drink, clothing, and money. And you cannot say that you didn't get it all from me: I gave you as much of it as I saw fit and now I don't want to give you any more. Do you know when you'd have been justified in complaining? If I had taken away from you more than I had given. Do you remember how many pleasures you enjoyed in times of prosperity? Pay me back what I lent you and let's be friends, like we were before. Don't you know that I have both noble lords and common men under my thumb, and I make them shiver with cold in June and swelter in the heat at Christmas? I give good things to some and bad to others, and I turn youngsters into old men.

"Tell me, what do you think of these high-interest loans?[17] In your judgment, are they taking a fair cut? For the bankers you know have converted gold into lead; and if you ask them 'Sirs, what do you owe me?' they will reply that they owe you a whole lot of love. They are not held in such high esteem as they used to be when the going was good and they were turning mercury into 23 carat gold. Today they would consider the account settled if they made a 50% loss—as there's neither trust nor truth—but they used not to be satisfied if they made 500 from

---

[17] Metge introduces a reference to the contemporary banking crisis. The Catalan word (*mogobell*) refers to a type of short-term loan with a punitive rate of interest (30% per annum) and a series of penalty clauses that were weighted heavily in favour of the lender. The Crown of Aragon had been taking out these loans during the 1370s to finance the royal debt, but in 1381, for a variety of reasons (including a reduction in income from Mallorca and a wider international economic crisis), defaulted on its—by that time—considerable repayments, leading to the collapse of the corresponding banking institution.

en fort breu temps, quan jo em volia.
Doncs, pus sabets que molt mal dia
vos puix dar, e molt bo, si em vull,
584 per què em guardats ab tan mal ull
dient mal de ma deïtat?
Per crim de lesa majestat,
si molt me fets, vos puniré,
588 e de tal verí vos daré
que no hi serà bastant triaga.»
«Na vella pudent, embriaga,
fets-me lo pijor que puscats.
592 Cuidats-vos, si bé em menaçats,
que per això reta la força?
Despullada m'havets l'escorça;
no hi resta sinó la rabassa.
596 Preg Déus tal gràcia me faça
que en breu la vejats dejús terra,
e puis en tota vostra guerra
ne en vós no daria un carlí.
600 Partits-vos corrent denant mi
e d'ací avant no em parlets.»
«Mon car amic, gran tort havets»,
dix ella, «com deits tals paraules.
604 Lleixem anar burles e faules,
car ja par que siats irat.
Digats, lo sol dóna clardat
tostemps al món, ne l'any calor?
608 Ne la mar ha tan gran amor
als navegants que aprés bonança
no els faça metre el cap en dansa
portant-los a perill de mort?
612 Dels hòmens me meravell fort,
qui em cuiden mudar ma natura.
Volets fer bé? No hajats cura
d'inculpar qui fa ço que deu,
616 car tot hom sap de cert e veu
que dar e tolre és mon ofici.
E doncs, posats vostre desfici,
car jo vull siats mon amic,
620 e fer-vos-he mil tants pus ric
e més honrat que mai no fos.»

20 silver coins in next to no time, when I wished it.[18] Now, since you know that I can either give you a very bad day or, if I fancy, a really good day, why do you look at me so askance and insult my divinity? If you keep on, I will punish you for the crime of lese-majesty, and give you such a potent dose of poison that no amount of antidote would save you."

"You foul-smelling, drunken old woman, do your worst to me. Do you think that I'm going to give in just because of all your threats? You've stripped the bark off me, and only the trunk remains. I pray that through the grace of God you may soon see that trunk buried: then you and all your warring would not be worth a penny.[19] Get out of my sight immediately, and never speak to me again."

"My dear friend, you are greatly mistaken," she said, "in what you say. Let's put joking and telling tales aside, because it now seems that you have lost your temper. Tell me, does the sun shine on the world all the time, or provide it with warmth throughout the year?[20] And is the sea so fond of sailors that after fair weather it never hurls them on, putting their lives in peril? I'm always amazed by those who think they can change my nature. Do you want to be fair about this? Then don't go blaming someone who is just doing what they have to, because everyone knows for sure, and can see, that my job is to give and take away. So, calm down because I'd like you to be my friend: I'll make you a thousand times richer and more respected than you ever were."

[18] The 'bankers you know' were Pere de Caus and his son-in-law Andreu d'Olivella, the two lenders behind the high-interest loans mentioned earlier. Metge, through the voice of Fortune, here draws a cynical parallel between their lending practices and the false science practised by alchemists who believed that lead was a metal ripe for converting into gold. He goes on to contrast their current desperate situation, now that their bank has gone under, with their previous practice when they lent 20 silver coins (Catalan *sous*) and got a return of 500 plus. Metge himself would have been well aware of the royal household's financial situation: his healthy salary would have been paid indirectly with the capital from these loans.

[19] A *carlí* (translated 'penny') is a coin of little value, probably named after Charles II of Navarre (1349-87).

[20] Here Metge switches briefly and seamlessly between his main source for this section—Settimello's *Elegia*—and the corresponding passage from Boethius's *The Consolation of Philosophy* (II, prose 2).

«Na vella vil, no ho veurets vós»,
dix ieu, «que daranant vos am,
624 car més me plau morir de fam
que si us havia a comportar:
car vós no us poríets estar
de tolre'm quant m'haguéssets dat.»
628 «N'arlot, pus així sots orat»,
dix ella, «tenits-vos per dit
que jo us metré en tan gran brogit,
en hora que no us cuidarets,
632 que tot ço del vostre perdrets,
jats que pauc vos n'haja romàs.»
E tornant-me prendre pel braç,
gità'm gran tros lluny del castell,
636 car no li semblà bo ni bell
res que li hagués fait ne dit.
E desparec-me ab tal brogit
que semblà lo cel ne vingués.
640 Dic-vos que lladoncs qui em trasqués
tots mos queixals, res no en sentira,
car ella em lleixà ab tanta d'ira
que els cinc senys corporals perdí.

644 APRÉS UN pauc ieu recobrí
mos senys, e viu vers mi venir
la plus plasent, a mon albir,
senyora que vui se despull.
648 Sapjats que ses beutats no vull
recitar particularment,
car sui cert que null hom vivent
les poria escriure ne dir,
652 e jo no vull tant presumir
de mi, qui son hom innocent,
que em tinga per suficient
de fer ço que altres no farien.
656 Ab esta senyora venien
set donzelles fort endreçades
e d'ornaments rics arreades,
però segons l'estil antic,
660 lo qual vui és gran enemic
de dones qui van per les cimes.

"You vile old woman," I said, "you'll not see me showing you any love from now on. I'd rather die of starvation than have to put up with you because you would not be able to stop yourself from taking away what you'd already given me."

"Scoundrel! As you continue to be such an idiot," she said, "you can be sure that I'm going to send such a disaster your way, just when you're least expecting it, that you'll lose everything I've given you, what little of it remains."

She then grabbed me by the arm again and hurled me a good distance from the castle, because she did not like anything I had said or done one bit. And she disappeared with such a tumult it was as if the sky were falling in. I tell you that if anyone had pulled out all my molars then, I wouldn't have felt a thing, because she left me with such anger that I lost all five of my senses.

However, after a short while, I recovered my senses and I saw coming towards me the most attractive woman in the world, in my judgment.[21] I am not going to list her attributes one by one, because I'm sure that no living person could tell of them or describe them in writing. And being an ignorant man myself, I do not want to presume that I am capable of doing what others cannot. Accompanying this lady were seven maidens, very elegantly turned out, and richly adorned, but in an understated, old-fashioned way, a style shunned by today's fuss-

---

[21] Metge's Prudence is modelled on Boethius's description of Philosophy in *The Consolation of Philosophy* (I, prose 1.1-3). In Alan of Lille's *Anticlaudianus*, the Liberal Arts construct a chariot to take Prudence to heaven (II.325-60). The allegorical figure representing Philosophy in Settimello's *Elegia*, Phronesis, is accompanied by the seven Liberal Arts (III.7). The episode that links the end of the narrator's dialogue with Fortune and his encounter with Prudence is not found in any of the main sources: it may be inspired by a passage in the *Remède de Fortune* by Guillaume de Machaut, a work that combined narrative verse and poems set to music, and which probably came to the Catalan-Aragonese court through the same channels as the *Romance of the Rose*, that is, through John I's wife, Yolande of Bar.

E jats que fossen assats primes
per llur cors e ben compassades,
664 semblà'm que fossen avançades
segons llurs cares en molts anys,
e que greus treballs ez afanys
haguessen sofert en llur temps.
668 E quan foren totes ensems
prop mi, qui bocadents jasia,
l'alta senyora qui venia
tan reialment acompanyada
672 tastà'm lo pols una vegada
e dix: «Est hom és perillós.»
«Senyora», dix ieu, «qui sots vós,
qui tan mal novell m'aportats?
676 Preg-vos mantinent m'ho digats,
ne si me'n porets ajudar.»
«Jo us en ajudaré, fill car»,
dix ella, «si molt vós volets,
680 car tal enfermetat havets
que lleu vos en poré curar.
Tots cells qui m'han volgut nomnar
Prudència díson vertat,
684 e si us tenits per consellat
de mi, tantost serets guarit.
Mes vull no gitets en oblit
d'aisí avant estes donzelles,
688 car si bé les vesets tan velles,
les pus excel·lents són del món,
car les set Arts liberals són,
qui de mi jamés se parteixen.»
692 «Senyora, en ma fe, bé mereixen
que per tot hom sien honrades,
e jur-vos que seran amades
per mi de bon cor mentre visca.
696 Soplei-vos que, ans que es desisca
l'arma del cors, me vullats dir
quin és mon mal, car defallir
cuid, si no m'ajudats en breu.»
700 «Mon fill, la malaltia greu
que havets ignorància és.
E si vós haguéssets après
com n'havíets avinentesa,

ily-dressed women. And though they were very slender and shapely, they seemed to me from their faces to be well advanced in years, and to have suffered serious trials and tribulations in their time.

And when they had all gathered beside me—I was lying face down—, the noble lady, who was so regally accompanied, took my pulse once and said: "This man is in a critical condition."

"My lady," I said, "who are you bringing me such bad news? I beg you, tell me at once, and say whether you will be able to help me."

"I will help you, my dear son," she said, "if you greatly desire it, because you are suffering from an illness that I will be able to cure you of with ease. Those who have seen fit to call me Prudence are quite right, and if you follow my advice, you will soon be healed. But henceforth I do not wish you to forget these maidens: rather aged they may appear to you, but they are the most excellent in the world because they are the seven Liberal Arts, and they never leave my side."[22]

"My lady, I do believe they well deserve to be honoured by all men, and I hereby swear to you that they shall be loved by me with all my heart as long as I live. I beg you, before my soul departs from my body, tell me what ails me because I think I shall die if you do not come to my aid very soon."

"My son, the serious illness that afflicts you is ignorance. And if you had learned your lessons when you had the chance, you would not

[22] In late-medieval schools and universities, the seven Liberal Arts inherited from the classical tradition (grammar, rhetoric, logic, arithmetic, geometry, music, and astronomy) provided the core curriculum that students mastered before going on to study the higher subjects of theology (or philosophy), medicine, and law.

704 no hàgrets faita la peguesa
en què vui havets dat del coll.
Fort me par siats estat foll
com a disputar vos sots pres
708 ab la bístia qui us ha mes
cent vegades lo cap al sac.
Bé us dic, però, que assats me plac
com l'havets bé desenganada,
712 car ella es té mal per pagada
de vós e de vostra paria.
E vei que de la malaltia
que sofrits ella n'ha lo tort,
716 e ha-us portat a punt de mort
ab falsa informació,
car vei que sots d'intenció
que ella us pot mal e bé donar:
720 açò no em podets vós negar
si volets atorgar vertat,
car, jats que us siats barallat
ab ella, jo en sé vostre cor.»
724 «Senyora», dix ieu, «per null for
açò que deits contradiria,
car, com ho faés, mentiria
per mig del caix, sal vostra honor.»
728 «Mon fill, vós ets en gran error»,
dix ella, «com açò cresets.
Obrits los ulls! E no vesets
lo cel, la terra e la mar?»
732 Lladoncs volguí'm en peus llevar,
ez ella em dix: «Prop mi siurets,
car la malaltia que havets
vei que us ha greument eclipsat.»
736 E quan tot ço que m'hac manat
haguí fait, ella em demanà:
«Mon car fill, sabets qui creà
totes les coses que mirats?»
740 «Senyora, vint anys ha passats
que en son tan cert com de morir
que les féu Cell qui volc sofrir
e per nós pres greu passió.»
744 «E doncs, pus ets d'opinió»,
dix ella, «que Déu creà el món,

have committed the crass error into which you've stumbled. It seems to me that you have been particularly foolish in your readiness to argue with that beast who has got the better of you a hundred times. I declare, however, that I am delighted with the way you have thoroughly deceived her, because she is displeased with you and with your company. And I see that she is to blame for the illness you are suffering from, that she has brought you to the point of death with false information: because I can see that you believe that she is able to administer good and bad. You cannot deny this if you wish to admit the truth: even though the two of you might have fallen out, I know what you really think of her in your heart."

"My lady," I said, "under no circumstances would I contradict what you say. If I did, I would be lying through my teeth, saving your honour."

"My son, you are greatly mistaken," she said, "if you believe that about her. Open your eyes! Do you not see the sky, the earth, and the sea?"

I wanted to stand up then, and she said to me:

"You will come and sit next to me, as I can see that the illness afflicting you has seriously affected your vision."

And when I had done as she had said, she asked me:

"My dear son, do you know who created everything that you see?"[23]

"My lady, for over twenty years now I have been as sure as I am of death that they were created by Him who was willing to suffer on our behalf, and who did indeed suffer a great passion for us."

"As you are therefore of the opinion," she said, "that God created

---

[23] From this point onwards, the debate between the narrator and Prudence follows the arguments presented in *The Consolation of Philosophy* (I, prose 6).

hajats per cert que cells qui són
per Ell creats fan ço que Ell vol,
748   e no poden contra son vol
fer, ne contra ço que Ell permet.
E doncs, si Fortuna us promet
mal o bé, com la podets creure?
752   Semblant m'és que assats puixats veure
que no ha poder absolut.»
«Senyora, jo em tenc per vençut»,
dix ieu, «d'esta gran qüestió,
756   mes prei-vos que em valla raisó
si la dic, e no us irescats.»
«Digats, mon fill, ço que us vullats,
que de mal e bé prou n'he vist.»
760   «Senyora, mon cor és pus trist,
ab menys esper que mai no fo,
car ab lusent provació
m'havets clarament demostrat
764   que ço que per Déu és creat
no pot res fer sens son voler
o Ell permetent. Així és ver
e ho cresec per lo sant baptisme.
768   Doncs, faç-vos un tal sil·logisme:
tot cell qui vol o permet mal
és fet a l'hom injust egual;
mes Déu, segons que havets provat,
772   permet fer molta malvestat;
doncs segueix-se que Ell és injust!
La conclusió menys que un fust
corcat val, car no és vertadera;
776   segueix-se, doncs, que la primera
o la darrera diguen fals.
A la major no digats àls,
car evident és, e fort clara;
780   doncs pusc-vos dir ab bona cara
que té falsa opinió
qui l'altra proposició
vol mantenir que vera sia,
784   car evidentment aparria
que de tot mal fos Déu la causa.»
«En est argument és enclausa,
molt amat fill, una gran nuu,

the world, you may be sure that those who were created by Him do what He wishes, and cannot act against His will, or against what He allows. So if Fortune promises you good or bad, how can you believe her? I think that you can see perfectly clearly that she does not have absolute power."

"My lady, on this important question," I said, "I admit defeat, but I beg you to understand that good sense assists me—if I have any—and I ask you not to lose your temper with me."

"Say whatever you wish, my son. I've seen my fair share of good and bad."

"My lady, my heart is filled with more sadness and less hope than ever, because you have clearly shown me, with brilliant proof, that what is created by God can do nothing against His will or without His consent. This is true and I swear by holy baptism that I believe it to be so. I therefore present the following syllogism to you:[24] anyone who wills or permits wrongdoing is no different from the unjust man; but God, according to what you have shown, allows much wrongdoing to be carried out; it therefore follows that He is unjust! This conclusion is worth less than worm-eaten wood, because it is not true. It follows, then, that either the first or the second premise is false. Do not dispute the first one, because it is evident and very clear; I can therefore tell you with confidence that whoever wishes to assert that the other premise is true, is quite wrong, because that would clearly demonstrate that God was the cause of all wrongdoing."

"My dear son, your argument contains a dense cloud,"[25] she said,

[24] A syllogism is a logical argument in which a conclusion is inferred from two related premises. Metge presents a categorical syllogism in which the conclusion ('God is unjust') is false, and infers from this that one of the two premises ('anyone who wills or permits wrongdoing is no different than the unjust man' and 'God allows much wrongdoing to be carried out') must also be false, in this case the second.

[25] Literally 'a great cloud' (Catalan *una gran nuu*), meaning a tricky theological problem.

788   car no es deu entendre tan cruu»,
dix ella, «com ho entenets.
Car la menor, que vós disets
que és falsa, dic altra vegada
792   que és vera e molt aprovada
per clergues e per sants doctors;
car, jats que Déu moltes errors
e malvestats permeta fer
796   e no cur sovent de refer
ço que serà mal ordonat,
sapjats que pura veritat
és, e fundament de raó,
800   que no consent que ab desraó
se faça res en aquest món.»
«Ara us dic que pus torbat son,
senyora, que jamés no fui.
804   Digats, què em direts d'aquest jui
que li vesem fer cascun jorn?
Que, en ma fe, quaix heretge em torn
quan vei que els bons soferen mal
808   e los malvats seen egual
dels prínceps e dels grans senyors,
ez han riqueses ez honors;
e puis, que els pobles los adoren,
812   e jamés no han mal ni ploren
ne saben què és adversitat.»
«Mon car fill, vós ets enganat»,
dix ella, «com imaginats
816   que haver grans honors e rictats
sia en lo món bé sobirà.»
«Cert, hoc, car l'hom qui res no ha
no hi és presat un fals pugès,
820   mes bé vei que a cell qui ric és»,
dix ieu, «tot hom li fa gran festa.»
«A l'hom ric, sabets què li resta,
mon fill?», dix ella, «Veure Déu.
824   Mes no hi és bastant ço del seu.
En açò no em contradigats,
car honors ne prosperitats
no fan paradís conseguir,
828   mes confessar e penedir
e complir los deu manaments.

"for it should not be understood as crudely as you have. The second premise, which you say is false, I say again that it is true and has been widely demonstrated by priests and by Doctors of the Church. For although God allows many errors and much wrongdoing to be committed, and often does not trouble to rectify the ensuing disorder, it is most certainly true and fundamentally right that He does not consent for anything to be done in the world without a reason."

"Now I tell you, my lady, that I am more confused than ever. Tell me, what are you going to say about this judgment that we see carried out every day? I swear I almost turn heretic when I see that the good are suffering, while the wicked are seated alongside princes and noble lords, and have wealth and honour; and furthermore, that the people adore them, and they never suffer any injustice, nor weep, nor even know what adversity is."

"My dear son, you have been fooled," she said, "if you imagine that having great honour and wealth is the ultimate good in the world."

"Yes, I may well have been," I said, "yet the man who has nothing is not worth a counterfeit farthing, but I can clearly see that the rich man is feted by all."[26]

"Do you know what the rich man lacks, my son?" she said, "He needs to see God. But his worldly goods are not enough for that. Do not dispute this with me: you do not get into Paradise through honour and wealth, but by confessing your sins, doing penance, and following the Ten Commandments. You know that good works are more pleas-

---

[26] The *pugès* (translated 'farthing') was a coin of French origin, minted in Catalonia between the thirteenth and fifteenth centuries, and of very little value.

E sabets que són més plasents
a Déu, qui és excel·lent bonesa,
832   les bones obres que riquesa,
favor ne honor temporal,
qui giten al foc infernal
tots cells que hi posen esperança,
836   car fan decantar la balança
comunament en greus pecats
e fan-los morir abcegats
per ço que no troben mercè.
840   E tots aquells que ab ferma fe
serveixen Déu, e lo món no,
jats que prosperitats no els do
en est segle, podets pensar
844   que els ho sap bé gasardonar
en paradís, car més los val
que en aquest món descominal,
qui fa damnar cells qui el serveixen.
848   Bé us dic que alguns són qui mereixen
honors e ricors temporals,
e ges dels gaugs celestials
per aisò no seran privats;
852   car Déu sap que no són pagats
quan vesen paubres famejar,
e no desigen mal usar
de les riqueses d'aquest món.
856   Mes, d'aquests tants, tan petits són
que no us en cal fer menció.
Pus ab clara provació
vos he mostrat, doncs, mon car fill,
860   que en béns temporals ha perill
a conseguir damnació,
falsa és vostra opinió
que en ells sia bé sobirà.
864   Vullats o no, vos covendrà
dir que Déu és sobiran bé,
car, segons que provat vos he
(e vós qui ho havets atorgat),
868   tot lo món fo per Ell creat;
doncs, si bé hic ha, Déu l'ha fet.
E sabets que és molt pus perfet
qui crea que la criatura:

ing to God—who is the epitome of goodness—than earthly wealth, favour or honour, which cast all who put their faith in them into the fires of Hell, because these things usually tip the scales towards serious sin, and lead people to die in blindness because they do not find mercy. And all those who, with steadfast faith, serve God rather than the world, though they might not be granted riches in this century, He knows how to reward them well in Paradise, for He is worth more to them in this unfair world that damns those who serve Him.

"I tell you that there are some who deserve earthly riches and honour, and who are not going to be deprived thereby of the joys of Paradise. God knows that they are unhappy when they see the poor starving, and they do not wish to abuse the wealth of this world. However, such people are so few in number that they are hardly worth mentioning.

"So I have clearly proven to you, my dear son, that earthly goods carry with them the risk of damnation, and that your idea that the ultimate good lies in them is a false one. Whether you like it or not, you are going to have to agree that God is the ultimate good because, according to what I have shown you—and you have acknowledged— He created the whole world. Therefore, if there is good in it, God has made it. And you know that the creator is far more perfect than the cre-

872 aquesta raisó no és escura,
que tot hom grosser l'entendria.
Doncs cell qui vol haver paria
ab Déu, sos mandaments complint,
876 no·l cal anar ab lo cap clin
si bé sofer adversitat,
car la pacient paubretat
és a Nostre Senyor plasent,
880 e cella li és desplasent
la qual hom sofer pel contrari.
Doncs ver és aquest correlari:
que sobiran bé és amar Déu
884 e que més val esser tot seu
que d'aquest món enganador,
e qui l'ama de vera amor
ab Ell per tostemps regnarà.
888 Segueix-se, doncs, que null bé ha
lo malvat hom, si bé és ric,
e que el bon hom, car és amic
de Déu, ha perdurable bé.
892 Molt amat fill, més vos diré.
Posem que gran felicitat
sia en est món esser honrat,
e que hom haja molta moneda
896 ab molts vestits d'aur e de seda
e res no·l venga pel contrari,
e que faça son adversari
venir en cell punt que volrà;
900 tot hom comunament dirà
que ço gran prosperitat és,
e que és dolent qui no ha res
e que viu en adversitat.
904 "Doncs", direts vós, "mal ordonat
és lo món com així és partit,
car molt aul hom vei ben vestit
ez ha diners e ço que vol,
908 e molt bon hom s'escalfa al sol
per tal com no ha què s'abric."»
«Senyora, certament vos dic
que, si és així com ho posats,
912 quants hòmens jamés foren nats
no me'n farien alre dir.»

ated: this is not an obscure argument, any simple man could follow it. So whoever wants fellowship with God, and is prepared to obey His Commandments, should not walk with his head bowed down in dejection, even in the face of adversity, because patient poverty is pleasing to Our Lord, and what is displeasing to Him is when man suffers it without patience.

"This corollary is therefore true: the ultimate good is to love God, and it is better to be all His than be deceived by this world. He who loves God with a true heart will reign with Him forever. It follows, then, that the wicked man has no goodness, even if he is rich, and that the good man, because he is a friend of God, has everlasting goodness.

"My beloved son, I will tell you more. Let us suppose that great happiness consists of being honoured in this world, of having a great deal of money and many clothes of gold and silk, of having everything turn out splendidly for you, and of being able to keep your adversary just where you want him. Everyone will usually agree that this amounts to great prosperity, and that whoever has nothing and lives in adversity is wretched. 'So,' you will say, 'the world is incorrectly ordered if it is thus divided, because I see many wicked men who are well dressed and have money and whatever they desire, while many a good man has to sit out in the sun because he does not have enough clothing to keep him warm.'"

"My Lady, I can assure you that if it is as you describe, all the men who had ever been born into the world could not make me contradict you."

«Ara vei que volets guarir,
mon dolç fill, de l'enfermetat,
916   car havets-me clar demostrat
l'entec que havets dins vostre cor.
E d'huimai no hajats paor,
que, Déu volent, guarit serets.
920   Vós, segons que jo vei, cresets
que cells que a vós dóna semblant
que sien honests hòmens han
aquelles virtuts que pensats,
924   e que cells que vós mal jutjats
sien injusts hòmens e mals.
E sabets que no són eguals
los juis dels hòmens d'aquest món,
928   car cells qui al vostre jui són
bons e honests e benfasents
seran mals al jui de les gents,
e pel contrari semblantment;
932   e no sabrets, per consegüent,
qual mereixerà mal o bé.
Pus llarg vos ho declararé
perquè en vejats mills la vertat.
936   Posem que sots tan endreçat
que los bons e els mals coneixets;
ges per això vós no saubrets
jutjar ço que mereix cascú,
940   car no és en aquest món algú
vertader jutge sinó Déu,
qui ab l'infinit saber seu
ço que fall a cascú coneix
944   e li fa segons que mereix,
tostemps pietat mejançant.
¿E no fon meravella gran
e jui de Déu fort amagat,
948   de Don Pedro, quan fo gitat
de Castella pel [rei] Enric,
e jats que ell fos potent e ric
e de son regne ver senyor?
952   Però Déu ne donà l'honor
a cell qui mal dret hi havia
a jui de la gent, qui disia
que l'Enric gran tort demandava;

"Now I see, my dear son, that you want to be cured of your ailment because you have clearly shown me the chronic illness within your heart. From now on, do not be afraid because, God willing, you will be healed.[27] As I understand it, you believe that those who appear to you to be honest men possess those virtues that you imagine, and that those whom you judge to be bad are unjust and wicked men. But be aware that the judgments of the men of this world are not the same; so those who in your judgment are good, honest, and generous, will be wicked in the eyes of other people, and vice versa. Consequently, you cannot know who is deservedly good or bad. I will explain it in more detail for you so that you can better see the truth of it.

"Let us suppose that you are so smart that you can tell the difference between the good and the wicked. But this does not mean that you will be able to judge what each one deserves, since in this world there is but one true judge, and that is God, who, in His infinite wisdom, knows what each person needs, and gives to each what he deserves, always with compassion. Was it not a great wonder, yet a well-concealed judgment of the Lord, when Peter was thrown out of Castile by King Henry, even though Peter was rich and powerful and the true lord of his kingdom?[28] But God bestowed the honour on the one who did not have the right in the eyes of the people, who were say-

[27] The following passage closely follows *The Consolation of Philosophy* (IV, prose 6-7).

[28] Metge illustrates Prudence's argument with an *exemplum* (illustrative anecdote) taken from contemporary Iberian history to show the gulf between human and divine judgment. In the second half of the fourteenth century, against a background of conflict between the monarchy and the nobility, the king of Castile, Peter I the Cruel (1350-69), is challenged for the throne by his illegitimate half-brother, Henry of Trastámara. With the support of the Crown of Aragon (Peter IV, 'the Ceremonious') and the backing of a French mercenary army, Henry succeeds in ejecting Peter from Castile in 1366. However, in the following year Peter regains the throne by defeating Henry at the Battle of Nájera with the help of Edward, Prince of Wales (the Black Prince). Following Edward's withdrawal, Henry defeats and assassinates Peter at the Battle of Campo de Montiel (1369) and is crowned Henry II. He repays his French patrons by becoming a staunch supporter of the House of Valois in the Hundred Years' War. Metge is updating a comparable *exemplum* from his source—Boethius's *The Consolation of Philosophy* (IV, prose 6.32-33), quoting in turn from Lucan's *De bello civili*—where the conflict was the Roman Civil War between Pompey and Caesar.

956 e finalment molt hom jutjava
que el rei Don Pedro era tal
que, si Déu no hi fos parcial,
son enemic del món gitara.

960 Los juis divinals, dic encara
que són tots fundats per raó;
mes són contra l'opinió
dels hòmens rudes, menyspresants

964 aquells, com no els veen semblants
d'aisò que ells n'han imaginat.
Molt hom serà per bo jutjat
segons lo món, e no volrà

968 fer males obres, e haurà
lo cor tan flac que, per ventura,
per alguna desaventura
que li vengués se lleixaria

972 del bé que començat hauria
e despuis faria tot mal;
e l'excel·lença divinal,
vesent lo cor d'aquest tan flac,

976 no li vol metre el cap al sac
per ço que no es lleix de bé fer.
Alscuns ne són qui llur esser
en Déu tan solament han mes;

980 ez Ell, qui veu que llur cor és
ab tan gran ardor acostat
a la santa divinitat,
no vol que sien agreujats

984 d'algunes greus enfermetats
que Ell donarà a qui li plau.
Alscuns ne són a qui la clau
del regiment del bé public

988 comana per ço que l'inic
sia punit del mal que fa.
Alscuns ne són a qui tolrà
gran part de llurs béns temporals

992 per ço que dels celestials
no sien per ergull gitats,
e vol que es tinguen per pagats
del mal o bé que els vulla dar.

996 Alscuns ne són que vol temptar,
e dóna'ls grans adversitats

ing that Henry's demands were wrong. And finally, many a man thought that, if God had not intervened, King Peter would have despatched his enemy from this world.

"Furthermore I say that all divine judgments are based on reason; but they go against the opinion of ignorant men, who denigrate them when they do not match the judgments they themselves have made. Many a man will be judged to be good by the world, and he will not want to commit wrongdoing; but he will have such a weak spirit that when, by chance, some mishap befalls him, he abandons the good works he had started and turns instead to wickedness. And God, in His divine excellence, seeing how weak this man's spirit is, does not wish to overrule him and so prevent him from doing good deeds.

"There are some who have entrusted their whole being to God alone; and He, seeing that their hearts have approached the blessed divinity with such intense devotion, does not want to burden them with serious illnesses that He can give to whomever he likes. There are some to whom He commends the keys of government, so that the wicked might be punished for their wrongdoing. From some, He takes away a considerable portion of their worldly goods so that they are not deprived of heavenly rewards through pride. He wishes them to be content with whatever He wants to give them. There are some He wishes

per ço que sien confirmats
per llur exercitació,
1000 que no hagen presumpció
de les virtuts que en ells seran.
Alscuns ne són qui guanyat han
lo regne de Déu per morir,
1004 car han volgut per Ell sofrir
pacientment molt vil escarn
e, noresmenys, que la llur carn
sia per infels destroïda;
1008 e volgren passar aspra vida
per bon eximpli a nós dar,
e que poguéssem veure clar
que més poden virtuts que mals.
1012 Mes dels hòmens qui no fan àls
sinó entendre en malvestats,
quan la gent veu que són plomats
e condemnats a crusel mort,
1016 no se'n meravella tan fort
com fa d'aquells qui no ho mereixen.
E puis, que dos béns se'n segueixen:
lo primer és car los malvats
1020 del mal que fan són castigats;
e lo segon, que s'espordeixen
tots cells que en fer mal s'atreveixen
quan vesen que als mals no pren bé.
1024 Mes vós direts: "Dona, bé sé
que si mals hòmens cerquen mal
e el troben, Déu és liberal
si els ne compleix llur voluntat,
1028 car, si troben ço que han cercat,
per contents se deuen tenir.
Mes què porets vós ací dir?:
molt hom injust mal cercarà,
1032 e Déu tant de bé li darà
com li poria demanar."
E jo us dic que em pens, mon fill car,
que el mal a qui Déu tant bé fa
1036 tan aul intenció haurà
que, si fretura el destrenyia,
en tals pecats declinaria
que el portarien a greu mort.

to tempt, and confront with great tribulations so that they might be strengthened by their experience, and not presume of the virtues they possess. There are some who have gained the Kingdom of God in the manner of their death: they have wanted to suffer patiently—in His name—most dreadful taunts as well as physical brutality at the hands of unbelievers; their desire was to live an arduous life and so set an example for us so that we might be able to see clearly that virtues are more powerful than vices.

"However, when people see those who do nothing but dedicate themselves to wrongdoing stripped of their wealth and condemned to a cruel death, they are not as amazed as when this happens to those who do not deserve it. And there are two benefits from this: the first is that the wicked are punished for their wrongdoing; and the second is that it terrifies all those who dare to do wrong when they see that wicked deeds do not pay. But you will say: 'Woman, I well know that when wicked men look for wickedness and find it, God is being generous in fulfilling their wishes; because if they have found what they were looking for, they should be content. But what can you say to this? Many an unjust man seeks out wickedness, and yet God bestows as much goodness on him as he could ask for.' And I will reply to you, my dear son, that I think that the wicked man on whom God bestows such goodness has such nefarious intentions that, if poverty compelled him, he would fall into such sinful ways that they would lead him to a terrible death.

1040   Alscuns ne són qui es temen fort
        de perdre llurs felicitats
        e guarden-se de malvestats
        per ço que Déu no els tolga res;
1044   e si bé lo cor d'aquests és
        humil ab mal entendiment,
        segueix-se'n un bé, car, tement
        que no vinguessen a fretura,
1048   lleixen lo mal e no han cura
        de fer los pecats que farien.
        Molts ne són qui degollarien
        per un florí tot son llinatge,
1052   e donen a tot hom damnatge
        ab que ells n'hagen algun profit;
        e quan ells han lo sac farcit
        e Déus ha vist que són tan alt,
1056   gita'ls d'aquí, e fan tal salt
        que es trenquen lo coll e la cama
        e perden quant han, e llur fama
        roman per tostemps denigrada.
1060   A molt hom malvat és donada
        potestat de la gent punir,
        e vós devets-ne presumir
        que es fa pels bons exercitar
1064   e per los malvats condemnar,
        car los sants qui sofrir volgueren
        per Déu crusel mort no hagueren
        corona d'aur aconseguida
1068   si doncs hòmens de mala vida
        no els haguessen llevats del món;
        e quan los malvats punits són
        cascun los pot gitar son llaix,
1072   car justament porten lo faix
        que llong temps havien cercat.
        Per què tenits per espatxat
        que Déu és jutge sobirà,
1076   e tot quant es fa ne es farà
        al seu voler és subjugat,
        lo qual és tan bé ordonat
        que no fretura de millor;
1080   e que tot hom té gran error
        qui es met en cor de mantenir

"And there are some who greatly fear losing their good fortune and refrain from wrongdoing so that God does not take anything away from them. Although their spirit is humble—for the wrong reason—a benefit follows from this: through fear of poverty, they eschew wrongdoing and strive not to commit those sins they were intending. There are many who would cut the throats of their entire family for a florin, and inflict harm on everyone else provided it benefitted them in some way. And when they have filled their coffers to overflowing and God has seen to what heights they have risen, He casts them down, and they suffer such a fall that they break their necks and legs, lose what they had, and their reputation is forever besmirched.

"Many a wicked man is given the power to punish people. You no doubt presume that this is done to exercise the good and condemn the wicked: after all, saints who wished to suffer a cruel death in the name of God would not have achieved their golden crown if wicked men had not first taken them from this world. And when the wicked are punished, everyone can revile them because they rightly bear the burden that they had long sought out.

"Therefore, you have it on good authority that God is the ultimate judge and that all that is or will be done is subject to His will, which is so well ordered that it has no need of improvement. Anyone who sets

que Déu a cascú fer ne dir
permeta, voler ni mirar,
1084 res que hom puixa imaginar
que sia fait ab desraisó.
Mes humanal opinió
aquests grans juis no pot entendre;
1088 per què no us en vullats contendre
d'ací avant ab hom vivent,
e, si us plats, cresets fermament
que Déu, qui és bé sobirà,
1092 lo món e ço que format ha
a bona fi ho volc crear.
E si volets considerar
del mal la definició,
1096 coneixerets que mai no fo
mal en est món, sinó tot bé.
La definició us diré:
mal és de bé privació.
1100 Doncs, no hi cal gran provació
que el mal que hom fa no sia res;
car privació res no és,
ne el mal que hom fa, per consegüent.
1104 Per què he provat clarament
que tostemps és bona Fortuna.»
«Senyora, mai persona alguna»,
dix ieu, «no ho creurà si lo hi dic.
1108 Quant és de mi, bé us certific
que no hi faria qüestió.
Doncs, major declaració
soplei a vós que me'n donets.»
1112 «Molt amat fill, vós los direts,
a tots cells qui volran dubtar,
que Déu l'ha volguda crear
per exercitar o punir,
1116 remunerar o corregir
los bons e els mals segons llurs mèrits:
los mals punir per llurs demèrits
e els hòmens bons remunerar,
1120 e els hòmens justs exercitar
perquè de si no presumesquen
e per ço que no s'atrevesquen
a mal corregir los injusts.

his heart on maintaining that God allows each person to do, say, wish, or see anything that one could imagine has been done without reason, that person is greatly mistaken. Nevertheless, the human mind cannot comprehend these great judgments, so you may not wish to dispute this with anyone in the future. And, if it pleases you, believe firmly that God, who is the ultimate good, wanted to create the world, and all He has given shape to, to good ends. And if you wish to ponder the definition of evil, you will discover that there was never wickedness in this world, only good. I will tell you the definition: evil is the absence of good. So there is no need of further proof that man's wrongdoing is nothing; since a lack of something is the same as nothing so, it follows, is man's wrongdoing. I have therefore clearly shown that Fortune is always good."

"My Lady," I said, "no one is ever going to believe this if I tell them. For my part, I assure you that I would not dispute it. But I beg of you an even more convincing argument than the one you have made to me."

"My dearly beloved son, to all those who doubt, tell them that God created Fortune to exercise or punish, to compensate or correct the good and the bad according to their merits: to punish the wicked for their shortcomings, to compensate the good, to exercise the just so that they do not become arrogant, and so that they do not err in their

1124 E tendran-se tots per vençuts
      cells qui el contrari mantenien,
      e veuran que res no sabien
      cells qui eren d'opinió
1128 que hom no els demostràs per raisó
      bona, lusent e vertadera
      que Fortuna jamés no era
      mala, jats que fos desplasent.
1132 E podets-los dir certament
      que Fortuna tostemps està
      en la mà de tot hom qui ha
      bon seny e raisó natural;
1136 car cella que jutjarets mal,
      si la prenets en paciença,
      vos darà clara coneixença
      de tots vostres defalliments;
1140 e, si en est món sofrits turments,
      paradís dellà consegrets.
      Mon car fill, pus entès havets
      clarament tot ço que us he dit,
1144 de l'enfermetat sots guarit;
      per què tornar-vos-en podets.
      E soplei-vos que em perdonets,
      car ocupada sui un poc.»

1148 E SEMBLÀ'M que ab falles de foc
      m'hagués hom donat per la cara,
      car no em volgra partir encara
      de la sua gran excel·lença.
1152 Ez [ella] ab fina benvolença
      acompanyà'm fins a la mar,
      e féu-me en la barca pujar
      ab què ieu era vengut aquí,
1156 e dix: «Donzelles, donats-li
      cascuna un plaisent besar.»
      Ez ieu volguí'm ajonellar
      ab cor que li besàs les mans,
1160 mes correc-me abraçar abans
      e besà'm fort honestament.
      E les altres encontinent
      ab cara rient m'abraçaren

correction of the unjust. And all those who maintain otherwise will be defeated. They will see that they knew nothing, those who thought that it could not be proven through sound, clear, and truthful reasoning that Fortune was never bad, no matter how displeasing she might be. And you can tell them with certainty that Fortune is always on the side of anyone who has good sense and natural reasoning. If you show patience in your dealings with her, whom you will judge to be bad, she will grant you insight into all your failings. And if in this world you suffer torture, you will achieve Paradise in the next.

"My dear son, as you have clearly understood everything I have told you, you are now cured of your illness and you may return. And I beg you to forgive me because I am rather busy."

AND IT SEEMED to me as if burning torches were being thrust into my face, yet I still did not want to leave the presence of her great excellency. With gracious goodwill, she accompanied me to the sea and helped me aboard the same boat in which I had arrived there. And she said: "Maidens, each of you bestow on him a pleasant kiss."

And I wished to kneel to kiss her hands, but she rushed forward to embrace me, and kissed me most chastely. And the others immediately

1164   e, burlant, la barca vararen,
       partint-se corrent denant mi.
       En tal punt que despuis no vi
       elles ne res que us haja dit,
1168   sinó que em trobé en cell partit
       en què fui al començament,
       quan la mar e el contrari vent
       me fasien lo cap rodar.
1172   Ez aprés pauc vau arribar
       al lloc on m'era recollit
       quan lo vilanàs mal vestit
       me trasí cautelosament.
1176   E la barca, sobtosament,
       a penes d'ella fui eixit,
       gità denant me tal cruixit
       que fo'm semblant tota rompés;
1180   e regiré'm, e no viu res,
       ne sabí si tenc bona via.
       Mes, ans que s'esclarís lo dia,
       per ço que no fos mal jutjat
1184   que tan gran maití em fos llevat
       e que m'anàs deportar sol
       (car no és presat un caragol
       qui no hic fa estat molt gran),
1188   torné-me'n ivaç passejant
       a mon hostal, dins la ciutat
       de Barcelona, on fui nat
       e morrai, si en sui cresegut.
1192   Ez ab aitant, Déu vos ajud
       e us don paradís aprés mort,
       car ieu no sai pus ric deport.

Finit

embraced me too, with smiling faces, and, joking all the while, launched the boat, and hastened away before my eyes. Suddenly I could no longer see them or anything I have described to you. Instead I found myself in the same situation as I was at the beginning when the sea and the strong headwind made my head spin.

After a short while, I arrived at the place where I had first boarded when that ill-attired villain had deliberately tricked me. Scarcely had I disembarked when the boat suddenly let out such a deafening crack right next to me that I thought the entire vessel had fallen to pieces. I turned round and could not see anything. I did not even know if I had had a good trip. But before daybreak, so as not to be poorly thought of for having risen so early and gone for a stroll by myself (as a man who does not make himself look important is valued less than a snail), I hurried back to my home, in the city of Barcelona, where I was born and where I will die, if I am to be believed. And with that, may God help you and grant you Paradise in the next life, for I know of no more precious delight.